Benjamin Capps and the South Plains: A Literary Relationship

Benjamin Capps and the South Plains:

A Literary Relationship

by Lawrence Clayton

TEXAS WRITERS SERIES

NUMBER TWO

UNIVERSITY OF NORTH TEXAS PRESS

TEXAS WRITERS SERIES NUMBER TWO

General Editor James Ward Lee

Printed in the United States of America
First Edition, 1990

The paper in this book meets the minimum requirements of the American National Standard for Permanence of Paper for Printed Library Materials, Z39.48-1984.

Library of Congress Cataloging-in-Publication Data

Clayton, Lawrence.
Benjamin Capps and the south plains : a literary relationship / by Lawrence Clayton.
p. cm. — (Texas writers series ; no. 2)
Includes bibliographical references (p.
ISBN 0-929398-09-2 : $19.95
1. Capps. Benjamin, 1922— . 2. Texas in literature. 3. Indians in literature. 4. Western stories—History and criticism.
5. Authors, American—20th century—Biography. 6. Authors, American—Texas—Biography. 7. Texas—Historiography. 8. Texas—Biography. I. Title. II. Series.
PS3553.A59Z62 1990
813'.54—dc20

89—70725
CIP

CONTENTS

INTRODUCTION

C.L. Sonnichsen says that Benjamin Capps writes "not better Westerns but better fiction about the West" ("New Style Western" 28). Certainly, Capps has varied from the traditional treatment of western material, emphasizing instead the conflict among the various cultures caught up in the continuous turmoil that characterized the settling of the West. He is fascinated by more than a century and a half of the mixing and mingling of various peoples and has found that cultural ferment a rich vein to mine as the basis for his writing.

Capps feels that fascinating people and events critical to the development of life as we know it are found in the annals of history outside the Indian wars and cattle kingdoms. He believes that writers have barely touched much of the subject matter that is available to the writer interested in the western United States and also believes that the traditional Westerns have overworked some phases of life there while ignoring others equally as important, especially from a human perspective.

Capps's books can be divided into three categories. Those dealing with the Anglo experience in the West from the early encroachment onto the Plains to the present are *Hanging at Comanche Wells, The True Memoirs of Charley Blankenship, The Trail to Ogallala, Sam Chance, The Brothers of Uterica,* and *The Heirs of Franklin Woodstock.* He has produced three works from the Indian perspective—*Woman Chief, A Woman of the People,* and *The White Man's Road*—all perceptive and sympathetic depictions of the life of the Indian in the West ranging from before white intrusion into Indian life to the early days of the twentieth century when Anglo domination changed forever the old ways of the Native Americans. In addition, Capps deals with Indians and whites in *The Warren Wagontrain Raid,* an unusual historical account of a raid by Kiowa Indians in North Texas near where Capps was later born and reared. Only the first of his books, *Hanging at Comanche Wells,* is even close to what most people think of as a traditional "Western."

The emphasis on characterization, historical background, and folklore makes these works perceptive studies of plausible characters in situations that demanded much of them physically and psychologically. This kind of material is the basis of good fiction, regardless of the setting. These books also demonstrate the diversity of Capps's interests and efforts. He is definitely not a writer of formula Westerns, and that penchant has perhaps cost him dearly in readership and critical interpretation, for Capps is an anomaly—a writer of quality or serious fiction set in the West. Had he written of similar conflicts east of the Mississippi, he might have been known as one of the great novelists in the United States rather than as a Western writer, a label that some feel suggests a writer of inferior quality.

Capps's attachment to the West is long-standing. Born in rural Archer County of North Texas on what was still in many ways the frontier, he grew up among reminders of earlier life represented by cowboys, ranchers, and the privations of rural living. These realities became strongly impressed on his mind. During his short career as a college professor in Oklahoma, he became acquainted with many young Indians from various tribes whose earlier exploits have fired the imagination of many writers, and he became intrigued by the names of these Indians and their reaction to the change forced on them by whites and white culture.

He traveled extensively over the West, taking notes on landscapes and people, and stored away these ideas to be used later in his books. He also read, widely and voraciously, about people and events all over the world. He saw what happened in the West as simply representative of similar activities in other parts of the world. So he adopted the West as his arena of exploration for the various situations with which life challenges people, writing of how some rise to the occasion and others succumb. Capps's laboratory of life has yielded a rich return to him and to those who read his works.

Capps's literary career seems to be prospering. Several of his earlier books are again in print from university presses, with his new novel, *The Heirs of Franklin Woodstock,* released in the Fall of 1989. The critical attention being given to him is heartening as well. Papers at professional meetings and articles interpreting his work have begun to appear more widely.

Capps is a man whose literary career has been devoted to the ideal of writing his own personal kind of books about the West, and he has managed to support himself as a professional writer. Although his output is small by comparison to some other writers—nine novels, three nonfiction books, parts of several other books, and an extensive body of book reviews and essays—no one can deny the quality of work that he has produced. Several of the volumes will likely be enduring classics as readers and students seek perceptive treatments of the life in the West. Capps's reputation as a serious interpreter of this life, not as a mythmaker or popularizer, seems secure, for he has indeed written "better fiction about the West" and is one of the best literary artists to write about the West.

1

CAPPS THE MAN

Benjamin Franklin Capps was born in the small town of Dundee, Texas, in Archer County on June 11, 1922, at a time when that part of North Texas was still part of the frontier that was struggling to move into the twentieth century. Capps's grandfather, a mustanger and cowboy, roamed West Texas during the 1870s catching and green-breaking horses to sell in Ft. Worth and other trade centers. Capps's father, also named Benjamin Franklin Capps, was born in a dugout in Archer County and worked as a cowboy in the area, breaking horses on the famous Waggoner Ranch near Vernon. As the frontier became more mechanized, the elder Capps also operated a filling station and worked in the oil fields, eventually becoming a driller. In 1917, Capps's father entered the army to fight in the World War. He came home, married, fathered three sons, and then died of a stomach ailment in 1926, at age forty.

Benjamin Capps's mother, the former Ruth Kathleen Rice, was the daughter of Will Rice, a frontiersman who had been a rancher, a real estate man, a part-time preacher, and for a short time a state senator from Decatur, Texas. Her grandfather, James Porter Rice, was a distant cousin of William Marsh Rice, founder of Rice Institute in Houston. Ruth Rice had taught school for three years at Uz in Montague County and at Holliday in Archer County before she married. After her husband died, she took her three young sons to pick cotton south of Wichita Falls. One son, six years old at the time, put his cotton in a burlap bag; Ben, four, put his in a flour sack; and the baby rode on his mother's long cotton sack.

Mrs. Capps was enterprising. As Capps remembers: "Besides all the money she made when she weighed [her cotton], momma got ten cents a day from men and women she carried to the cotton patch in our good Model T, whether they rode inside or had to hang onto the running board" ("Lifetime of Lessons" 44A). Realizing the need to support her family through the winter, she secured a teaching job in Anarene, a town eight miles south of Archer City. Anarene was on the railroad and had once done a thriving business, but when the main highway was paved in the late 1920s and oil helped replace coal as the fuel for trains, Anarene fell on hard times and, like many other such villages, disappeared.

The Anarene school had two rooms, one serving as

a classroom and the other as the home of Mrs. Capps and her three sons. Capps's earliest recollections are not those of deprivation and loneliness. Instead, he remembers a mother who cared for her three sons and encouraged him to become an avid reader. "She was a remarkable woman," Capps says. Years later he would recall: "She was a pioneer in small schools in the days before orange busses and consolidated schools, and she became a pioneer in special education, a program to help 'exceptional' children. Maybe she started her interest in handicapped students in Anarene. She had two pupils who were mentally retarded and a Spanish-American grown woman, in the first grade, who had epileptic seizures" ("Lifetime of Lessons" 44A).

Life was hard in Texas in the 1920s and 1930s, but Capps recalls that like other families they kept a garden, a cow, an orchard, and a flock of chickens and guineas to help supplement modest incomes and provide items not readily available in the grocery stores of the day ("Eating Well in Lean Times" 38A).

The ranch country of north central Texas furnished Capps with his most lasting education, and although his life drew him far from the region, he was never unaware of this part of Texas and the kind of life he had known there. As Lou Rodenberger states in her review in *Western American Literature,* Capps seems never to have considered his past in any way except as a chapter in the history of northwestern Texas and western Oklahoma (262).

His apprenticeship to writing about life in the West began at an early age, for he saw much of life, including cowboys and ranch men daily, and began to store memories for use later. He also recalls entertaining—or scaring—his brothers with stories he made up in their upstairs, unheated bedroom—stories about a great white ape, huge African snakes, and drums beating in the night. His creativity was at work here to break the boredom of this life. He recalls his early years in an interview with newspaperman and novelist C.W. Smith: "I never lived in a house with electricity or running water until I was sixteen. We used to walk to a neighbor's house to listen to the radio, the Grand Old Opry. Our horizons were much more limited in those days. We'd walk to the post office or ride horseback there once a week, and so books were important to us" (8).

Capps started his education early because he lived in the school building, and, at the age of fifteen, graduated as salutatorian from Archer City High School in 1938. He spent his first summer after graduation delivering soft drinks on a Double Cola route that led him through Lorenzo, Ralls, Crosbyton, Dickens, Spur, and Plainview on the edge of the Texas Great Plains and its ranching and farming country. His pay was seventy-five cents a day and his meals.

Capps left his native north central Texas to enter college that fall at Texas Technological College (now Texas Tech University) in Lubbock, where he had received a small scholarship for writing an essay on his reasons for attending Texas Tech. In an interview, he said that he wanted to be a writer, but he thought, "Well, I can't be a writer. I am not from New England and the South wasn't very big in those days, so I was a long ways from being a writer." Capps thought he might study law, but friends and relatives persuaded him to study agriculture, which was becoming scientific and which seemed to be a promising field. He entered the course without enthusiasm. In a letter to Ernest Speck, on November 3, 1978, he recalls some excellent courses in English, chemistry, and botany, but he has seen little good from his courses in dairy manufacturing and poultry husbandry.

The Great Depression made life hard for most Americans, and for many college students it was a matter of "working your way through." Capps has said he nearly starved to death. He worked his way through by sweeping classrooms for the National Youth Agency, run at that time by the young Lyndon Johnson. But, despite his best efforts, Capps was forced to drop out of college after the first year. He left Texas Tech in midsummer of 1939 and joined the Civilian Conservation Corps. From 1939 to 1940 he became what was called a "tree monkey" or CCC Boy and was sent to Colorado to work. In 1940, he was discharged from the Corps and got a job surveying for the U.S. Corps of Engineers at Grand Junction, Colorado. His pay was thirty-six dollars a month.

In 1942, with the United States at war, Capps helped survey for an airport at Greenville, Texas, and on his twentieth birthday he took the aviation cadet test in Dallas and passed. He had to wait eight months to begin active duty, so, during the interim, he took a job driving a dirt mover on the crew building Lake Texoma, a federal project on the Texas-Oklahoma state line. After an accident that resulted in a broken collar bone and clavical, a fractured skull, and three cracks in his pelvis, Capps spent thirty-seven days in the hospital. His injuries further delayed his entering service, and he and his fiancée, Millie Marie Thompson, to whom he had become engaged while working in Colorado, decided to marry. When Capps recovered, the two were married in Ardmore, Oklahoma, in 1943, just ten days after Marie's sixteenth birthday. Recovered from injuries sustained in the accident, Capps entered military service and, after training, served from 1943 to 1945 in the Pacific theater of war. He flew forty missions as a navigator of a B-24 and attained the position of flight navigator with the rank of first lieutenant. His unit, Seventh Air Force, 11th Bomb Group, 26th Squadron, saw action at Kwajalein and Truk Atolls, at Jaluit, and at Wake Island. They later bombed Yap, Iwo Jima, Chichi Jima, and Haha Jima.

After the war ended, Capps joined the wave of veterans who returned to college with their expenses defrayed by the G.I. Bill. Determined to get the best training in writing then available, he resumed his education at the University of Texas in Austin because he had heard that they had a good writing program. There he had an outstanding career, being elected to Phi Beta Kappa and earning his bachelor's degree in 1948.

At the University of Texas he began a long and sometimes frustrating formal apprenticeship to the craft of fiction through creative writing courses. While a student, he wrote short stories for the student-edited literary magazines at the school, as well as about sixty unpublished stories. These were not Westerns but dealt with his earlier life, including his war experience. One of his stories appeared in the first postwar issue of *The Ranger*. He contributed a column in the *Daily Texan* titled "Bull Session," a section that gave veterans a chance to air their views (Stowers, "Benjamin Capps," 25). In addition, he wrote a large number of news items for the *Daily Texan.* He did three pieces for *Lariat Story Magazine:* "Tom Horn—Lawman and Renegade," "Kid Curry and the Wild Bunch," and a piece on cattle brands from the early Spanish brands to the widespread illegal practice of brand altering. He also wrote "Blind Man's Bluff" and "The Second Best Navigator" for the *Texas Literary Quarterly* in 1948. The second story won third prize in a creative writing contest in 1949. He won an honorable mention for "The Man without a Son" in the Texas Book Store Contest and first in an essay contest for "Buckner's Reef" in the Spring of 1946.

Capps's first fiction piece sold to a magazine, *Sir!,* was "Uncle Rufus and the Cat-Scratch" in 1949. The same year he won a first and a fifteen-dollar prize for "Ruthy," a short story he did not publish. In 1963 he placed "The Last Bearden" with *Alfred Hitchcock's Mystery Magazine,* a suspense publication. He wrote some of these early pieces to fulfill course requirements. He also wrote a factual article on the use of open refrigeration units in grocery stores, a new idea then, and sold it for thirty-eight dollars. His classes were paying off.

He has fond memories of Dewitt Reddick, a journalism professor at the university. He recalls that newsman Walter Cronkite said he had learned everything he knew about journalism from Reddick.

Capps also studied under Harry Ransom, his adviser in the English department, and he took three conference courses in creative writing under Ransom. Since he was interested in both journalism and fiction writing, Capps says he probably took more writing courses in his college career than anybody else ever did.

Having shown a penchant for success in formal education, Capps continued his work at the University of Texas and received his master's degree in 1949. Instead of doing the usual critical or interpretive thesis, Capps, encouraged by internationally known folklorist Mody C. Boatright, did a creative thesis—a novel dealing with life as he knew it in Texas in the 1920s. Capps completed the work, titled *Mesquite Country,* but despite repeated revisions has been unable to place the work with a publisher. A chapter of the work, "Slim Wilkinson," has been published in *Horsing Around: Contemporary Cowboy Humor,* a collection of work by Curt Brummett, Paul Patterson, Elmer Kelton, John Erickson, Baxter Black, Sam Brown, and others. He produced three other unpublished novels: *Ethel May, Movers of Earth,* and *Hell, Fire, and Drinking Water.*

Capps acknowledges his debt in this and other areas to Boatright, whose specialty was western American folklore, folklife, and literature and recalls that Boatright encouraged him to continue writing fiction about the Southwest. Several letters between the two indicate a warm teacher-student relationship continuing for several years, and Capps dedicated *The Trail to Ogallala* to his former professor. Boatright's early encouragement, along with the advice of an English teacher in junior high school to write about what he knew, convinced Capps of the direction his career should take.

At this point, however, Capps took a job teaching English and journalism for two years at Northeastern State College in Tahlequah, Oklahoma. Capps did not take to the academic life and felt ill prepared to do all the work that he had been assigned, particularly a heavy load in journalism that included sponsoring the school paper. He came to believe that an academic career was more harmful than helpful to a writer, or at least it was to him (Lee, "Benjamin Capps" in *Fifty Western Writers,* 43).

Capps left his teaching post in 1951 and moved his family to Paris, Texas, where his mother owned a house left to her at the death of her second husband, Millard Martin, a rancher whom she had married in 1930. Capps thought the house in Paris would be a good place to try his hand at writing full time. He wrote extensively on a novel titled *Movers of Earth,* a story based on his experiences on the Lake Texoma project. He prepared a chapter outline and perhaps twenty thousand words of the novel itself. Even though he was unable to interest a publisher in the piece, his apprenticeship was being served.

Once more, economic necessity entered his life. With his savings exhausted and his wife expecting their third child, Capps moved the family to Grand Prairie, between Dallas and Fort Worth, Texas, where he has lived since that time, except for a few months when he lived at the site of the socialist colony called La Reunion in West Dallas. He began a career as a tool-and-die maker because he thought such work would be sufficiently different from writing fiction and would not drain his creativity. His idea proved incorrect, however, and he failed to produce as much creative material as he had hoped during the ten years in machine work. He still was determined, however, to be a writer. In 1961, he left his trade as a tool-and-die maker to write full time again.

In 1962, *Hanging at Comanche Wells* was published by Ballantine Books, an outstanding publishing house for Westerns at that time. Capps had found a field that would prove fruitful for his labors—the South Plains of Texas, the general area where he had lived for much of his life (Dunkelburg 1D). James Ward Lee notes that this novel "is not a success, for it falls somewhere between the formula western and serious fiction, but it is not a complete failure either." Lee believes that the novel shows

Capps's "ability to tell a story in an interesting and coherent manner and demonstrates his talent for creating characters" ("Benjamin Capps" in *Fifty Western Writers,* 43).

Capps's productivity saw a surge in the next decade or so. His output during this time includes the following novels: *The Trail to Ogallala* in 1964, *Sam Chance* in 1965, and *A Woman of the People* in 1966, all by Duell, Sloan and Pearce of New York. Then *The Brothers of Uterica* was issued by Meredith Press in 1967, *The White Man's Road* by Harper and Row in 1969, and *The True Memoirs of Charley Blankenship* by J.P. Lippincott in 1972. In addition to the novels, Capps also published *The Indians* from Time-Life Books in 1973, *The Warren Wagontrain Raid* by The Dial Press in 1974, and then a second book in the Time-Life series, *The Great Chiefs* in 1975.

Capps wrote sections of three different editions of Fodor's Travel Guides and many essays. In 1964, he wrote "A Critical Look at a Classic Western" and, in 1969, a three-part piece titled "The Promise of Western Fiction" in *The Roundup,* the organ of the Western Writers of America, of which he is a longtime member. He also wrote, in 1973, "Breaking into Print" and, in 1974, "Overture to Ogallala," both of which also appeared in *The Roundup.* Another essay, "Mama, Bill, Roy & Me," a touching portrait of his early years at Anarene School, appeared in the "Southwest Letter" section of the *Dallas Times-Herald* in 1981. In 1982, he wrote "Eating Well in Lean Times," a study of how families lived in those difficult days, and a year later, "Building Tanks for Stock Raised Appreciation for Clean Water," both also in the "Southwest Letter." In 1984, he contributed "Lifetime of Lessons" to the "Southwest Letter," a piece that deals mostly with the experiences of his mother and the admiration he held for her.

In order to make a living, he did free-lance writing and contributed well over one hundred reviews of books principally about the West, for the *New York Times*, the *Dallas Morning News*, the *Dallas Times-Herald*, and the *Fort Worth Star-Telegram*. He also contributed to journals and magazines such as *Western American Literature* and *Saturday Review of Literature*.

Capps's career has been handicapped because, unlike many successful novelists, he has been unwilling to help promote his work. He refuses to make speeches, although he has agreed to appear on discussion panels. A good example of his reluctance to speak involved an invitation by Ernest Speck to speak in 1974 to the annual meeting of the Texas Folklore Society, an organization in which Mody Boatright had been prominently active. In a letter dated August 20, 1973, Capps told Speck that he would speak on the material he had gathered to write *The Warren Wagontrain Raid* and would speak "as an amateur historian" who has been working on a Texas subject, not as a folklorist. In a letter dated September 1, 1974, however, he says, "Finally I have decided that I should not accept the invitation, even though . . . I have great respect for the group and would be highly honored." He goes on to say "I have about three or four opportunities before me to make speeches and intend to say no to all of them. To be very frank, I am just not a public personality. It costs me somewhat more psychologically than it does some people; in other words if I have such a date something nags at me off and on constantly until it is done. A couple of weeks ago, I went on a TV show in Fort Worth, and I didn't get a whit of writing done for two days before the date."

Capps has not isolated himself from his chosen profession. As chairman of the screening committee for the Spur Awards for Western Writers of America, he served with Kenneth Fowler, Natalee Kenoyer, and Don Worcester. In addition, he assumed the position of writer-in-residence at the University of Texas at Arlington for the Spring and Summer of 1976. It was at this time that he felt he should leave behind the western set in the past and "write some contemporary novels" (Hart 1).

One of his projects while employed at the University of Texas at Arlington was to help edit a collection of works by Duncan Robinson, longtime professor at the school. The volume, titled *Duncan Robinson: Texas Teacher and Humanist,* was coedited by Thomas Sutherland and was the first book published by the press at the university. In addition to editing the work, Capps contributed a major portion of the "Introduction." In 1977, the library at this school bought one-third of his papers and materials for a "nominal sum," and he put the rest of his materials there on loan (Capps, letter to Ernest Speck, 6 March 1978).

One of Capps's traumatic experiences involves a case in which his work was blatantly plagiarized. Although Capps is forbidden by terms of the settlement to speak on the matter, Mary Simpson completed a master's thesis at North Texas State University in Denton in 1986 titled "Benjamin Capps and the *Sacajawea* Plagiarism Case." The summary of the information given in her first chapter indicates that the book in question was *Sacajawea* by Anna Lee Waldo, published by Avon Books in the Spring of 1979. Simpson characterizes the book as one of those "fat, historically based novels with much descriptive narrative" (1)—and "fat" it was indeed, at 1,408 pages. The book sold well, but within five years after its publication, plagiarized passages were found from twelve books, including Joseph Conrad's *Lord Jim,* Jack London's *Call of the Wild,* and James Michener's *Hawaii,* as well as four novels by Capps: *A Woman of the People, The Trail to Ogallala, Sam Chance,* and *The White Man's Road.* Other writers whose work had been plagiarized included John Steinbeck and Frederick Manfred.

Although the effort to secure justice and file suit was to disrupt his life for nearly two years, Capps launched into it with serious intent. He hoped that the case would cause the legal community to take greater pains to see that this kind of theft did not occur again. The case ended with a stipulation in an Order of Discontinuance of June 22, 1983, that the amount of money awarded to Capps would never be revealed. It is known, however, that Frederick Manfred received $4,200 as his part in an out-of-court settlement. A second edition of *Sacajewea,* issued at a later date, claimed to be an expanded version, even though, Simpson notes, the book actually was shorter. Many of the plagiarized passages were deleted or greatly altered, and documentation was provided for others. The action ended an interesting but frustrating period in Capps's life.

In 1990, all of Capps's work is in print or under consideration for reprint, except *Hanging at Comanche Wells.* This situation is an improvement over previous years. In 1984, for example, Ernest Speck wanted to use some of Capps's novels in his Southwestern Literature class at Sul Ross State University but could not find in print the books he needed. Shortly thereafter, the presses at the University of New Mexico, Texas Christian University, and Southern Methodist University brought out quality reprints of several of his books with afterwords by scholars in the field, thereby ensuring that his works will remain in print for years to come.

In his books Capps has carved out a niche for himself that few others have achieved. Recognition for his work has been encouraging. For *The Trail to Ogallala,* he won the Spur Award from the Western Writers of America for Best Western Novel of the Year and the Levi-Strauss Golden Saddleman Award for the best western writing of 1964. This book was also selected by the National Association of Independent Schools as one of the ten best books of the year for precollege readers. It was, as well, one of thirty-one novels selected that year for inclusion in the White House library by the American Booksellers Association.

In 1965 his third published novel, *Sam Chance,* won him a second Spur Award, and in 1969 *The White Man's Road* gained Capps his third Spur Award, a record matched by few other writers. For this same book he also received the Wrangler Award of the Cowboy Hall of Fame and Western Heritage Center in Oklahoma City for the best western novel of the year. In 1972, *The True Memoirs of Charley Blankenship* was among three finalists for the Spur Award, a degree of recognition also gained by *Woman Chief* in 1980. The Wrangler Award of 1974 for best western book of nonfiction went to *The Warren Wagontrain Raid,* a book that was also one of three finalists for a Spur Award that year. Thus, six of Capps's books either won or were in the finals for this prestigious award.

Further recognition by his peers in the state came from his election to the Texas Institute of Letters in 1967. In 1986, he was awarded Honorary Life Membership, the highest award given by the Western Literature Association, an organization of scholars from across the United States and some foreign countries who are dedicated to the interpretation of the literature of the American West.

Although he did not publish a major work between *Woman Chief* in 1979 and a contemporary Western, *The Heirs of Franklin Woodstock,* in 1989, he has been engaged in many writing projects, including a long philosophical essay. Even if he produces nothing else, Capps's reputation as a writer of serious material about the West is secure. His readership is not found in the same ranks of those who read the work of Zane Grey, Louis L'Amour, and other popularizers who produce formula fiction. Rather, Capps attracts readers interested in interpretive work that sheds light on such issues as right versus might, ethnic relationships, human conscience, and brotherhood, all classic themes in American letters since the time of James Fenimore Cooper, who in *The Pioneers* created the pattern for the Western.

Exciting adventure is certainly a part of Capps's work, but the emphasis is on character development, not action for its own sake. Capps should be remembered as one who has chronicled the real life of the West, not as one who prostitutes one or two select groups by glamorizing their activities—real or supposed—in an effort to sell books. In his review of *The True Memoirs of Charley Blankenship,* Speck says that Capps has written "honestly and well about a segment of American life" (152).

Capps's West is as real as we in this day will ever see it because Capps has researched, thought about, and recorded life as he has come to understand it from the fairly primitive existence and experience of his childhood in rural Texas. According to William T. Pilkington, one of the most productive and perceptive scholars of Southwestern life and literature, Capps has proved "that it is still possible to take a fresh and interesting view of some well-worn subjects" (12).

2

THE ANGLO NOVELS

Capps wrote six novels dealing primarily with the experience of Anglos at various periods in the settlement of the West, principally in Texas: *Hanging at Comanche Wells* (1962), *The True Memoirs of Charley Blankenship* (1972), *The Trail to Ogallala* (1964), *Sam Chance* (1965), *The Brothers of Uterica* (1967), and *The Heirs of Franklin Woodstock* (1989). Four of the novels treat the period from just after the Civil War through the trail drives and the settlement of the frontier; one is about the founding and demise of a socialistic agricultural commune located in present-day Dallas; and one focuses on the contemporary West.

Capps's grasp of the events, problems, and people who were involved in settling the West is apparent in his able depiction of life on the frontier, his accuracy in describing the settings, and his portrayal of diverse characters. The quality of writing in all but one of these novels—the apprentice work *Hanging at Comanche Wells*—is representative of Capps's work generally. A plausible, direct style of presentation and a strong emphasis on historical accuracy and folklore of the culture depicted also characterize these novels.

Hanging at Comanche Wells

Capps's first published novel, *Hanging at Comanche Wells,* is a short law-and-order novel set around 1883 in a small frontier Texas town. Capps has admitted that he based his story on the experiences of Tom Horn, the well-known frontiersman, deputy sheriff, former Pinkerton detective, and later killer-for-hire for cattlemen in Wyoming in the late 1890s and early 1900s. The narrative is not told from Horn's point of view, but does emphasize the kind of crime for which Horn was eventually executed in 1903, the murder of William Nickell, the fourteen-year-old son of a sheepherder. Capps changes the age of the boy, who was probably mistaken by Horn for the lad's father, from fourteen to twelve and the setting from turn-of-the-century Wyoming to an earlier day in Texas.

This is Capps's only published attempt at a "popular" Western, and even it is in some ways atypical of that somewhat amorphous genre. The book too much emphasizes psychological considerations and philosophical issues such as the conflict between right-versus-might to be a true "powder burner." The novel does, however, mix a number of elements associated with the traditional Western—cattle rustling, murder, gunfights, fist fights, Texas Rangers, cowboys, a school marm, and the like.

The cast of characters is appropriate for such a book. The protagonist is Bart Youngblood, a deputy to Sheriff Bell, a strong and highly motivated upholder of law and order. The principal force in promoting the power of the law is Judge Albert Pendergrass. Albert has been crippled since age twenty-eight, when a falling mustang crushed one of the man's legs against a rock. The judge is a dedicated servant of the law, even to the point of siding with those against secession of Texas from the Union during the Civil War. Because of that stand, he has been relegated to an obscure judgeship in remote West Texas while his former associates have prestigious appointments in Austin and other important places. The evil element in the novel is represented partly by Stephen Pendergrass, the brother of Albert, owner of the huge Rail P Ranch and a former president of the powerful Cattleman's Association. The blatantly evil element is represented by William Ivey, a former army scout, deputy, and later lawman turned hired killer.

The central question probed in the novel is whether the sheriff and judge will be able to convict

Ivey and then keep him in custody until the scheduled date for the hanging or whether the cattlemen will break him out of jail to prove that they still control life in the frontier town of Comanche Wells. The situation parallels that of Stephen Crane's "The Bride Comes to Yellow Sky," for both works view a town at the time when the lawless frontier is being overcome by the forces of law and order so that the next era of civilization can hold sway.

Albert makes his point when he tells Stephen that the man who paid Ivey to kill the suspected rustlers has "turned loose a monster in this country" (130). The characterizations are somewhat stronger than is typical for the popular Western. Youngblood is a fallible young man who nonetheless whips a much larger and stronger cowboy in a fist fight, manages to keep Ivey from escaping, and generally handles himself and his young wife well. He is wounded in a gunfight but does not let that or the blow Ivey gives him on the head keep him out of the ensuing action.

The only other strongly developed figures in the book are the Pendergrass brothers—Stephen, the violent one who feels driven to control the ranch country, and Albert, the formerly active man who is forced into a sedentary occupation by an accident that leaves him with a crippled leg. Stephen Pendergrass is an obnoxious, overbearing man whose wealth has given men like Ivey a chance to kill.

Pendergrass is a stereotypical overbearing banker, as well as the owner of a large ranch; thus, he combines two roles often found in a traditional Western. He uses his role as banker to control the former sheriff by not foreclosing on an overdue loan the ex-lawman owes the bank. Pendergrass has a large house on the ranch with a library and other finery and a wife that he has cowed into obedience, but he is not the cultivated person he tries to imitate. His dominating desire is to continue to control the life of Comanche Wells, and he particularly dislikes his crippled brother's success in bringing law and order to the town, as symbolized by the conviction of a man that the cattlemen support. He even calls Albert a cripple in an effort to belittle him after repeated efforts to bribe, berate, and denigrate him, especially by labeling Albert's judgeship insignificant and paltry.

The reader gains insight into Stephen's true nature when Albert notes that Stephen's claim of having fought in the Battle of San Jacinto during the war with Mexico is false. Albert reminds his brother that the boys were teenagers at the time and that Stephen got a whipping from their father when he returned from the battle because Stephen had not planted the corn his father had instructed him to plant.

Capps's picture of a representative of law and

order, Albert, as a cripple is symbolically appropriate. The accident that left him unable to walk normally turned an active man—actually Stephen's superior in many ways—into a contemplative man, one who was forced to become bookish and decided to study law. The metaphor is an apt one, though perhaps a little obvious for the sophisticated reader.

The climax comes with the attack on July 31 by a group of thirty-seven carefully chosen riders led by Stephen Pendergrass himself mounted on a huge black horse and wearing a black hat. He is the Angel of Death, he thinks, and with some reason, for he has the power of life and death over many people. Bledsoe, one of the ranch leaders, is arrested when he rides up to Sheriff Bell under a flag of truce during the attack and is imprisoned in town in a cellar. As in many Westerns—*High Noon* and *High Plains Drifter,* for example—the townspeople must decide whether to rise up and help the beleaguered legal officials. The defense of the town by sixteen men including the sheriff's men, four Texas Rangers, Lieutenant Ruth, and several armed citizens is successful. Although the defenders take some casualties, such as Eb, the old blacksmith who is killed, they realize that repulsing the attack breaks the back of the cattlemen's effort to control the town. Several leaders of the cattlemen's cause are killed, including Underwood, a supposedly pious Baptist rancher who nevertheless instigated the attempted jail break by Giles. There is little doubt by this time that the execution will take place.

The execution does proceed as the judge had decreed—in full view of the populace on the appointed day and at the announced hour. Law and order have come to Comanche Wells. Ivey's savage resistance on his way to the gallows is for naught, and he is dragged, literally kicking and screaming, to his punishment. The scene is interrupted only by the killing of Stephen Pendergrass by Juan Torres, a mysterious Mexican gunman and a friend of Ivey's, who puts five bullets in Pendergrass's chest and the last one in his head from no more than two feet away, all while on horseback at a dead run. After Ivey's body is cut down, the sheriff orders the gallows torn down.

The plot is complicated by the pregnancy of Youngblood's wife, Lela. She spends part of her last month of pregnancy on the ranch of Youngblood's uncle, Charlie Moss, who was on the jury that convicted Ivey and obviously sides with the forces of law and order. But Lela's plight is exacerbated by the long hours her husband has to work to thwart efforts by cattlemen to free Ivey. The two young people have a strong relationship and a supposedly typical one—Youngblood is a former cowhand with three trips up the trail and a bunch of tomfoolery to his credit; Lela is a former school teacher who surprised Youngblood when she accepted the shyly offered proposal of marriage. Youngblood intends to return to the Moss Ranch to be foreman for the uncle who raised him after he was orphaned at an early age during the Civil War. The conviction of Ivey causes him to stay on an extra month because the sheriff needs the help and Youngblood does not want to be known as one who quits in a crisis.

The closing scene seems a little trite—the baby born to the Youngbloods at that time is named Albert after the judge, and Youngblood himself decides to study law, rather than return to the life of a cowboy as his uncle's foreman. But as is true in some of the best literature, order is restored. A major step toward ending the frontier lawlessness has been made in Comanche Wells.

The appearance of the mysterious Mexican, Juan Torres, is a somewhat unusual twist in the story. A gypsylike figure, he floats in and out of the action and provides suspense by being an unknown factor, suspected by both sides as being in league with the other. Why he makes no effort to free his friend Ivey is unexplained. Perhaps he saw it was impossible to do so, but he may also have seen that Ivey was guilty and therefore let justice take its course. He did, however, see to the punishment of Stephen Pendergrass for not making good on his promise to protect Ivey.

Especially for a first novel, *Hanging at Comanche Wells* is not a poor work. Sonnichsen guardedly calls it "reminiscent of *The Ox-Bow Incident*" ("New Style Western" 27). Many writers would gladly claim it. But for Capps it was an apprentice work, a trial balloon, a novel that he finally sold. It did draw him to the setting that he would depict in most of his fiction, the American West in the latter nineteenth century.

The True Memoirs of Charley Blankenship

The True Memoirs of Charley Blankenship is a medium-length work in the open-ended picaresque tradition of Mark Twain's *The Adventures of Huckleberry Finn.* The protagonist is very much the picaro, for he wanders around the American West from 1880 to 1890 in close contact with a representative melange of particularly well-drawn frontier character types who provide interesting adventures during the latter days of the open-range frontier. Charley's efforts to find his brother, Buck, are at least as much his own effort to "see the elephant and listen to the hoot owl prowl" (12).

In the novel Capps covers much the same range of frontier activities that he does in *Sam Chance,* although in *Sam Chance* he confines the arena of action largely to Texas. In *The True Memoirs of*

Charley Blankenship, he ranges over a much broader canvas of western landscape, from Missouri to Texas, Wyoming, Arizona, New Mexico, Colorado, Nebraska, and points in between.

Blankenship sets out with his worldly goods in a tow sack. Like Benjamin Franklin walking the streets in Philadelphia, Blankenship is off on a new adventure but with six ears of corn he parches for food, not three loaves of bread, as Franklin did. The trek to Texas with an unscrupulous man and his sick wife, six ill-mannered children, two wagons, a reluctant milk cow, and poor food sets the tone for much of Blankenship's additional adventures. By the time he has endured his experiences with a crew gathering bones of every description (even human ones), a band of psychopathic stage robbers, various groups of cowboys, buffalo hunters, and other ne'er-do-wells, Blankenship has been tested and tempered and his base of experience stretched beyond what many could endure. But Blankenship is still a tyro, susceptible to the next tutor. His success may have been due, at least in part, to learning to "keep [his] eyes open, [his] mouth shut, and grin a lot" (44) to cover up his lack of skills and knowledge.

His picaresque experiences provide the humor in the novel. Some of the humor is ironic, as in the case of Mr. Crankshaw, the loafing freeloader on the buffalo range, and some is of the rough-and-tumble frontier type, such as the episode involving the bucking horses and Red Paden. This latter kind of humor is sometimes characterized by one's facing difficult circumstances and even being seriously injured. The humor derives from the audience, who enjoys not having to face the difficulties of the one suffering, and is the basis for much cartoon humor. The shivaree of the young couple seems in a class all its own, so outrageous are the antics.

One interesting area of his expanding awareness is Blankenship's education with females. When he and his friend Jake go on a spree in Dodge City, Jake offers Blankenship some homespun philosophy by pointing out that a man has to agree before he can be fleeced by the cheap whores and gamblers that prey on the cowboys there. Blankenship has trouble understanding Jake's advice at first but realizes that in order to be taken in by such activities, he has to agree to participate in them. He takes the information to heart and initially avoids being taken in by a barfly named Lillian. Later, however, she fleeces him out of eighty dollars in the role of "weeping Lil," who claims she lost all of her belongings and money in a fire that Blankenship helped fight most of the night. She says that she has been saving the money to go back home and lead a respectable life. Blankenship holds his own by resisting Lil, until she asks him to feel a feverishly hot bruise on her thigh.

Later, Blankenship gets drunk, and lust drives him to Lil's boarding house; but she is gone. Enraged, he disturbs the peace and is hit on the head when he resists arrest by the town marshall. The judge turns him loose after a sound lecture, and Blankenship rides west. Years later, Blankenship finds Lil running a saloon. She does not recognize him at first, though she thinks he might be several other people she pulled the same trick on. She claims to have returned the money—the only such case of remorse causing her to send money back after she tricked a man out of it. Charley believes her story but wonders if he has been tricked again. He is reminded of Jake's advice and realizes that he must admit that he let Lil get by with her scheme. He just laughs as he rides on.

At the end of the novel, Blankenship realizes he cannot resist the West. He says, "Coming home for a visit was the best thing I'd done in a long time, but the land out there was too big, too full of possibilities and opportunities, too full of interesting people, to turn my back on. Besides that, I was too good a cowhand to give up the business" (252). Blankenship eventually owns a ranch in eastern Colorado, and, by 1909, when he supposedly wrote the manuscript, he was also managing his father's farm in Missouri. In this book, Capps brings into play three noteworthy literary traditions. The "true memoirs" technique was used as early as 1720 in Daniel Defoe's *Memoirs of a Cavalier*. Capps's "Introduction" claims that the manuscript was written in 1909 on paper made from "wood pulp, quite cheap, and today brittle" (9). Capps hedges against inaccuracies by claiming that "the ink has faded to a dim sepia color, hardly distinct from the hue of the browning paper." He then insists, for the sake of plausibility, "that the present version is as accurate as reasonable care and patience and persistence can make it" (9).

The structure of the novel is obviously picaresque with the journey as the structural vehicle. The unity in the novel is provided by Blankenship's periodic recollections of home, especially his buying a bracelet for his mother and in his eventual return home. Blankenship's coming full circle with Lil also provides an element of unity, as does the introductory note describing the scope of the supposed manuscript.

The *bildungsroman* element in the tale is obvious, for this is Blankenship's growing into awareness. At the end of the narrative he says that he "would not give back a single bruise I got wandering around in the West" (252). Life hurts sometimes, as we learn, but Blankenship is willing to pay the price for experience.

Capps states his moral at the end of the book: "Human critters have a strange mingling in them, of sunshine and shadow, of goodness and meanness, of sense and nonsense. They are a mystery, but they are all we've got. Do not harden your heart, nor get too set in your mind about them" (252).

Telling the story through Blankenship's own dialect accomplishes for Capps what Twain's use of Huckleberry Finn as narrator did for the American humorist in his famous book—it allows the personality and folk nature of the narrator and the material to come through in grand style and humanize as well as humorize the piece. The reader gets Blankenship's thoughts and feelings far better in this format than would be possible from other points of view.

The universal implication of the story is apparent in the quest that each of the three Blankenship brothers undertakes. The older one, "Buck," as he prefers to be called, goes out West and later returns home, much impressing his young brothers and firing Charley with the desire to "go west." Later, when Charley, who opts for the name "Duke," returns after years of looking for Buck, he discovers that Buck is farming not far from his boyhood home where the older brother lives with his wife and children. The youngest brother, Pete, who has adopted the name of "Ace," has gone in search of Charley. Charley sums it up when he says "That Pete! Ace! Running around out there thinking he was looking for me. Maybe the young whippersnapper was looking for himself, or maybe he was looking for a dream" (251). Probably he was looking for both, but Blankenship reveals in this perception the truth about his own wanderings.

Capps's insistence on historical accuracy is supported in the "Introduction" for he indicates his intention to present Blankenship as a "typical American cowboy":

> First he ran away from a farm on the eastern edge of the Great Plains, which region, from Minnesota to east Texas, provided a large percentage of the skilled labor for western ranching. Second, he worked in a number of the famous old-time ranching areas: along the Powder River in Wyoming, in the Tonto Basin in Arizona, along the Pecos River in New Mexico, and for large ranches in northwest Texas such as the Matador and the XIT. Third, he ends his story not upon some climactic event in his own life but appropriately, though probably unconsciously, at the time of his first return home in 1890, which is the year symbolic of the closing of the American frontier. (10)

The accounts of Teddy Blue Abbott, Andy Adams, and Charles Siringo, all firsthand recountings, bear out the accuracy of Blankenship's experience and equipment, even to the saddle that he buys, the double-rigged style commonly used by Texas cowboys.

The clothing is no less authentic: Justin boots, John B. Stetson hat, and Levi jeans and jacket.

The folk elements in the novel are ably woven into the fabric of the narrative in an unobtrusive way. The frequent use of proverbs and folk expressions that serve as Blankenship's touchstones with reality also humanize him and reflect his continuing naiveté. Capps's technique is often to credit the folk with the proverbs by introducing them with "as they say": "Like they say, God tempers the wind to the shorn lamb" (64), or "No use fishing in troubled waters, as they say" (73). The folk expressions are usually metaphors and similes familiar in the western lexicon: "Lord-a-mercy; it was hot as a two-dollar pistol out there today" (25); "The sun burned down hot as a depot stove" (19); "He buffaloes me" (61); "Even Elmo tried to cotton up to me" (80).

The narrative is smoothly executed with ample humor, action, and characterization. Blankenship is certainly one of Capps's most interesting figures, even if he is naive throughout most of the adventures. The history, folk elements, and representative activities mark this as an outstanding historical novel.

The Trail to Ogallala

Although the practice of driving cattle long distances from South Texas to market or breeding ranges to the north ended after a relatively short period of time, writers have been unable to leave the experience alone. Like Custer's annihilation at the Little Big Horn to Indian buffs, the trail drive is a magnet to the imagination of those interested in the cowboy. It was, no doubt, an important factor in the development of the frontier because it brought money to Texas and made some people rich. It took into a new world the men otherwise isolated on the Texas frontier and changed their lives, as revealed by the views of many of them in J. Marvin Hunter's *The Trail Drivers of Texas,* and it created a folk figure that embodies the stuff of myth. Although many novels use the trail drive as a peripheral occurrence, not many focus on it exclusively.

The Trail to Ogallala is Capps's effort to produce a novel completely out of a trail drive. The central figure is Billy Scott, a fine twenty-eight-year-old cowboy with more than a dozen years of experience in the cattle business and a natural leader among his peers. The time is 1880, and Scott has been given the job of trail boss over a herd of two thousand longhorn steers and a thousand cows to be driven from the Lawson Ranch southwest of San Antonio to Ogallala, Nebraska, a developing cattle area located between the North and South Platte Rivers. It is an arduous journey through West Texas and on up through Indian Territory, across western Kansas, and into western Nebraska.

When Scott and his two friends, Cory and Shorty, drive a small herd of Spanish heifers into the gathered trail herd at the Lawson Ranch, they are surprised to learn from Greer and Brown, co-owners of the herd with Lawson, that Lawson has died and that his widow, unaware of her husband's prior commitment to Scott, has hired Colonel Horace Kittredge, an experienced trail boss and a family acquaintance from Georgia, to take charge of the herd. Scott determines to quit but is persuaded by Brown and Greer to stay on with the promise that he will be the foreman on the ranch if he chooses and will definitely be in charge of the trail drive the following year.

Capps was well aware of the tradition of the trail drive novel and admits being especially conscious of two predecessors—Andy Adams's *The Log of a Cowboy* and Emerson Hough's *North of 36*. In an interview he said that he strove to be "more deliberate than Adams, more realistic than Hough." In a letter to Mody Boatright on March 23, 1964, Capps says, "I guess I'm taking a risk in this book, following as nearly as I do the same general material as Andy Adams's *The Log of a Cowboy*. What I was hoping to do was to write with the same authenticity of detail, yet come up with distinctive characters and more of a fictional organization of a story than Adams had." Capps knew he was competing against a host of other predecessors: Zane Grey's *The Trail Driver,* Mel Marshall's *Longhorns North,* Jim Bosworth's *The Long Way North,* as well as Ray Hogan's *Passage to Dodge City,* Clay Fisher's *The Big Pasture,* and another Adams book, *The Outlet.*

Capps also admits to being aware of the fictional use of nature as a hostile force, such as is seen in Jack London's "To Build a Fire," but he knew that nature could also be good. He realized that in his epic quest he was paralleling the drive with the hunt of the whale in Melville's *Moby Dick.*

Capps's success is unarguable. As Boatright says in a letter to Capps, "I have said that it would be hard for any writer to follow Andy Adams with a realistic trail driving novel, but you have brought it off very well" (April, 1963). Characterization is one of Capps's strongest skills, and one finds early in *The Trail to Ogallala* that Capps has given attention not only to creating interesting characters but to diversifying figures in his novel. Boatright comments to Capps in his letter, "Your characterization of Scott, Kittredge, and Blackie is especially good, and your Professor furnishes a fine chorus."

Capps is obviously interested in making his main characters appear as far more than stereotyped cowboys. Their backgrounds are diverse and their abilities varied. They represent a valid cross section of men on the frontier—Civil War veterans, an educated man, a Mexican with a past tainted by murder, a cantankerous cook, a young wrangler, and a host of other figures representative of the time and place.

A good example of this character development is found in Captain Horace Kittredge. In fashion typical for him, Capps takes us into the mind of Kittredge as he contemplates the men he has on the trail drive:

> Cruel war had done its share to shape his manner. He had seen men die and their goals not reached because of vacillation in their leaders. Also, perhaps, he had come to consider the lives of men and the efforts of their days not too precious. He was concerned about the condition of the herd and of the trail. (Ace edition, 76)

He continues his musing:

> The individuals working under him he had already estimated much more than any of them suspected. As a whole, he considered it an average outfit, adequate to the job if they were handled properly. All of his thoughts, as he ranged far out along ahead of the herd, were concerned with the task he was in charge of, the natural obstacles, his plans for the weeks

> ahead, sometimes the men he would use in fulfillment of his plans. (76–77)

Other characters are developed by varied means. For example, Scott, the central figure in the story, is depicted through his own thoughts and actions but also through the thoughts of Kittredge. Other parts of Scott's background are filled in by the narrative. We learn that he is a veteran of working with the archetypal trail drivers, Charles Goodnight and Oliver Loving. He failed to realize that "he, Scott, the kid, had no idea that he was part of something that would be remembered forever by men who raised cattle. For his whole boy's heart and soul had been saturated with the simple desire to please Mr. Loving, to show that he could be a good cow hand to do his part" (98). He learns from experience: "When you have done your best, you are not satisfied with losing any at all. When you start to do something and find that it is harder than you thought, you try harder, and the goal is made precious by the work and sacrifice and pain that go toward it; and you are never satisfied with losing any at all" (98).

Richard C. Poulson praises the novel by saying that "Capps . . . cultivated the ability to see both cows and cowboys as characters, individuals both functioning together, equally independent on one another to make the drive. The tension, for example, of a stampede is thus more meaningful because of the tension of the novel, a tension between two sets of characters playing each other against a hair-fine balance called going up the trail" (60).

In his seminal piece of criticism in *Southwest Review,* Don Graham notes that the principal difference between Andy Adams's treatment and Capps's is in the development of characterization and the stock solutions to problems normally depicted in popular western fiction. For example, Scott avoids the typical solution to the problem represented by Blackie, which would have been to shoot him, as Scott's companion Cory even insists that Scott should do. Graham goes on to praise Capps's treatment of Scott who "undergoes a very convincing psychological growth." Scott is "a man drawing his strength from a rich heroic tradition sympathetically felt and rationally perceived. What Scott learns is the difference between ability and maturity. Specifically he learns the difficult circumstances under which ability receives a sterner test than mere practicality." Graham goes on to say that part of what Scott has learned on the drive is that some "obstacles were not fair. Not fair at all" (302).

One of the reasons that Scott is such a powerful figure is that his situation is classic. Capps admits that he had in mind, for example, a similar situation with the Greek hero, Achilles, who in the Trojan

War was a leader and warrior of incredible proportion, but who was not in charge. James Ward Lee recounts Dobie's comment that Adams's *The Log of a Cowboy,* the book frequently compared with *The Trail to Ogallala,* was the best that can be written about cowboy life. Lee then suggests that *Trail* is better for several reasons: "Capps is a much better writer than Adams, but what is most important is that while Adams went on a drive and turned his trip into a narrative, Capps imagined a trip, and, as Aristotle pointed out, literature is superior to history" (*Classics of Texas Fiction* 14–15).

The most recent piece of fiction begging comparison with Capps's novel is the Pulitzer Prize winner *Lonesome Dove* by Larry McMurtry, who is, like Capps, an Archer County native. McMurtry's novel is far longer and more complex, with its several subplots and numerous characters, but it does not focus on the trail drive as the central concern—on stampedes and the reasons for them, on the fatigue and the dust-choked life of the trail driver, on the influence on life of poor-quality horses, and on the development of individual animals. McMurtry emphasizes instead the often romanticized aspects of trail driving and other adventures experienced on the way. Capps's work is far more directly focused on the experience of the drive itself.

The folk element in the book in quite strong, not

so apparent as in *Sam Chance,* but skillfully woven into the fabric of the tale. The most obvious use is the journey motif of the trail drive as well as the drive itself—the procedures for handling cattle in this kind of operation. These traditional techniques are learned from others or from experience. They are so necessary as to become traditional. Scott, for example, had learned his from Goodnight and Loving. Blackie had not learned from anyone.

The singing of folk songs and the practice of singing to the cattle show the influence of folklore. Scott sings "Barbara Allen," a legitimate folk song, but the other men sing such popular hits as "Dixie" and religious songs like "Nearer, My God, to Thee" and "Amazing Grace" (110). The Kid plays "Turkey in the Straw" and "Buffalo Gals" on his harmonica. The actual practice of singing to cattle has, of course, been widely discussed, but firsthand accounts bear out the practice and the benefit of it—settling the cattle—so that they are less likely to be startled by the sudden appearance of a rider or other outside noises.

In typical Capps fashion, this novel weaves the factual, the folkloric, and the fictional into a tapestry of the Old West in its heyday in a controlled, carefully shaped novel that ranks Capps at the head of the class in this kind of fiction. By using an imagined drive, Capps was free to choose plot elements necessary to communicate the experience while focusing at least equally on characterization, which, as Rodenberger notes in "The 'Gen-u-wine Stuff,'" separates this novel from the host of others (10).

Sam Chance

One of the most comprehensive of Capps's novels is *Sam Chance* (1965) for it follows the career of the title character from 1865 until after the turn of the century. Rodenberger calls it "the most perceptive chronicle exploring that evolution of the Civil War soldier into Texas cowboy and finally cattleman who became a legend in his own time" ("The Novel of the Cowboy" 528). The plot of this full-length novel opens as the Civil War grinds to a close.

The focus of the work is indicated in the title—the book is a study of the life and accomplishments of Sam Chance, an early-day cattleman. Chance is similar to Charles Goodnight, the pioneer cattleman in Texas, but the story of Sam Chance is not a retelling of the life and experiences of Charles Goodnight. In a letter to Mody Boatright on July 12, 1965, Capps responds to the notion that Sam Chance is heavily patterned after Goodnight. He first cites differences between the man and the fictional character: "Actually . . . Goodnight was not from Tennessee, was not in the regular Confederate Army, came to Texas long before 1865, [and] did not ranch in the same area as my fictional Sam Chance." Capps also notes that Chance "did not drive cattle over the Chisum or Fort Griffin–Dodge City Trails." He does point out some similarities, however, and admits that they were "actually more than I had intended." Capps laments that he did not put into the story everything that he might have included: "It seems to me that I should have written a much longer story, spelling out the details of his wife's life, of his good-for-nothing buddy's life, his children's experiences, a more fair account of the nester, etc., but then again it occurs to me that it is all implied in the book already." In a July 21, 1981, letter to Ernest Speck, Capps admits that he may have "overloaded the evidence" in Sam Chance's favor. He says, "A big cattleman might have a few unusual virtues. Goodnight and Waggoner did sympathize with the Indians. Littlefield did donate library money (as well as fountains). Some big rancher was intellectual enough to become an early president of Texas Tech. Granville Stuart did feel loyalty toward his employees. C.C. Slaughter did donate the money for a hospital in Dallas, but I load all of these kinds of virtues on one man and then not only show him out-guessing the weather and the cattle market, but predicting the dust bowl. Also, Chance is . . . too much the polemicist, too articulate." He admits in the same letter that Sam Chance, along with Woman Chief and Billy Scott may "have too much heroic stature."

As a person, Chance changes little in the course of the novel. He is throughout strong-willed and physically able, but he lacks the human qualities of concern for the feelings and mental fragility of his wife. He is too much concerned with the demands of his vigorous outdoor life. Capps has depicted the hero who married, a step that tradition says will betray his heroic proportion. Capps illustrates the problem for the wife, a problem common to frontier women, who found life more than they could cope with. Chance's family was a handicap to him, but not much of a hindrance to his work and routine, which demanded that he be gone for long periods of time. The situation was common on the frontier, and, along with the harsh climate and danger, is what made this life more than some could tolerate.

The basic pattern of *Sam Chance* parallels Homer's *Odyssey,* in which the warrior leaves the battleground and launches on a long journey filled with adventure and hardship. Capps extends his narrative far beyond that of Homer, but the episodes of danger, the scope of the setting, and the nature of the conflict with various antagonists certainly seem similar in tone to the classic story.

In addition to being an outstanding novel, *Sam*

Chance is also an accurate historical study of activities on the frontier from the days of hunts for wild cattle through the coming of the railroad and the arrival of civilization and the founding of schools, towns, and the like. Capps's depiction of the buffalo hunting is certainly accurate, including Chance's early feeling that buffalo hides could be made into usable leather despite the white man's inability to process the hides effectively, even though the Indians could. Later, tanners perfected the process for softening the buffalo skins, and the market for the skins became enormous. The massive and well-organized buffalo hunts such as the one depicted in the novel became commonplace until the late 1870s when the buffalo herds on the Texas ranges were decimated.

The same statements about accuracy can be made of the depiction of trail drives in the novel. Although the accuracy of Capps's depiction can best be (and is) discussed in conjunction with *The Trail to Ogallala,* the point needs to be made that this novel reflects perceptive understanding of the history and techniques of this undertaking. As an examination of the history of the livestock industry in the American West will show, Capps also accurately depicts the practice of overgrazing range land. Even though cattlemen could easily see that grangers would ruin the country by plowing it up, they failed to see that they themselves were endangering the fragile ecology of the region by overstocking the ranges.

As Capps depicts, the coming of the railroad did more perhaps than any other development to change the nature of the frontier. It effectively ended the need for long cattle drives, and it also brought to the region people who produced goods that then needed to be transported to markets. So with the railroad came more people, towns, schools, and the other accoutrements, both positive and negative, associated with civilization.

Water may be the most precious commodity in West Texas. Capps has Sam Chance voice this concern, and it is indeed a pressing one. Water is the essential ingredient to ranching, although some would cite grass as being primary. Without water, cattle cannot survive at all. In periods of drought and low forage production, cattle can survive on hay. They cannot, however, survive without water. Industrial development necessary to a strong economy in a civilized area also depends heavily on water.

Chance's trouble with Indians is representative of the time, even to his being troubled by them in his earliest explorations along Silver Creek. The Indian raid on the cow camp is certainly plausible, and his punitive raid is no less historically typical. The response of the Indians is expected, for they were a warring people who did not respect Chance's benevolent act of returning the horses. Their image of fair play was to take what one was strong enough to take and not to apologize for the action.

The battle between the Indians and the buffalo hunters also is accurately represented. Details resemble, for example, the actions at the Second Battle of Adobe Walls, where a group of buffalo hunters using long-range Sharps .50-caliber rifles thwarted a massive attack by mounted Indians. Although Capps has modified details, the broad scope is similar.

Other instances of Capps's accurate representation of the events and milieu in which his actions occur could be cited: the portrayal of the surrender of Confederate forces to the Union, the trip to the river trading center of Jefferson in far East Texas, and others.

One of the most obvious of Capps's historically accurate incidents is the major die-off of cattle on the open plains during the bitter winters of 1885–1886 and 1886–1887, a time that historians of the period generally acknowledge as the end of the open range period. This disaster hit not only Texas but most other parts of the American Western grazing lands as well, forcing ranchers to fence their range lands and control the breeds of cattle that ran on that land. Hence, the end of the use of formerly wild longhorns as breeding stock gave way to cross-breeding, first with Durhams and then with Herefords and other British breeds, and led the way for the increased use of cross-breeding and pure-bred animals of various breeds now populating the grazing lands of the American West.

The pattern of settlement is accurately represented as well. The typical sequence was for explorers and later hunters to travel the land and then for cattlemen to begin to make use of the grasslands. The buffalo hunters cleared the land of the bison and left it available for grazing by cattle. With the coming of the railroad, increased numbers of people brought civilization to the frontier with the foundation of towns and the institutions associated with it: churches, schools, families, various businesses, and legal codes that brought an end to the open range and frontier freedoms.

Another piece of historically accurate detail is Martha's response to life on the frontier. A good illustrative example highly praised for its accuracy is Dorothy Scarborough's novel *The Wind,* in which the relentless wind drives insane a young woman from Virginia trying to cope with life on the dusty prairies. Walter Prescott Webb in his history of the Great Plains says, "Much of the evidence . . . reveals that the Plains repelled the women as they attracted the men. . . . If we could get at the truth we should doubtless find that many a family was stopped at the edge of the timber by women who refused to go further" (505). Then he says, "The loneliness which women endured on the Great Plains must have been such as to crush the soul, provided one did not meet the isolation with an adventurous spirit" (506).

Although folklore does not play a major role in this novel, the patterns are certainly present. Ways of performing various occupational tasks are accurately represented. Even though Capps had history to draw upon to reveal these patterns, Anglos in the area learned how to hunt and skin buffalo, for example, from those with experience just as they had learned the secrets of cow hunting from those who were involved in that early-day activity.

The techniques of trail driving, such as how to handle the herd, how to keep direction by pointing the wagon tongue at the North Star each night, how to handle meals, and the like, are no less based on folklore, for although individuals worked out these techniques, these were picked up and followed by others who learned them from word of mouth, not from books or formal education.

The skill of tracking and determining how much time had passed since the tracks had been made certainly fall into the category of folklore, and Chance learns from Lemon, the cow hunter, that night crawlers, so-called because they do not crawl during the day, reveal whether the tracks were made before daylight by the presence of their own marks in those tracks.

Frontier folk groups are well represented in the novel—vaqueros, buffalo hunters, cowboys, Indians, merchants—all seem "right" for the setting in which Capps places them.

The speech of the characters in the novel is quite representative with the appropriate wording such as *remuda* for the herd of horses on the ranch and other instances such as the use of "bob" wire for "barbed" wire, still a fairly common pronunciation in this area. One must agree that Capps certainly has a good understanding of the folklore of the area and era about which he writes.

If one were to fault *Sam Chance* as a novel, it might well be the episodic nature of some of the final sections. The subject—the settlement of the northwest Texas frontier from the early coming of Anglos after the Civil War through the coming of the railroad—may include too much time to cover in one tightly structured novel. In *Sam Chance,* Capps works with how the protagonist faces change as well as how the situation in which he functions changes and how in turn that alters the perspective of those with whom a person must deal. If the individual is unable to change, and it seems customary to expect that he cannot, then the attitudes of people toward him will change. One sees the same flaw, for example, in

Elmer Kelton's *Eyes of the Hawk,* a novel quite similar in pattern and scope to *Sam Chance;* nonetheless, the book is one of Capps's very best and is quite different in setting and type of activity from the next one.

The Brothers of Uterica

Sonnichsen's comment on the quality of Capps's books "about the West" is nowhere more evident than in a non-Western, *The Brothers of Uterica,* a full-length work. Written from the first-person point of view, the novel relates the experiences of a colonist named Langly, a former Methodist minister and teacher, who is exploring the possibility that socialism is the answer to his dilemma of finding a rewarding life. In the end, he discovers that this route does not provide the answers he seeks.

The central figure of the narrative, if one looks past Langly, is Jean Charles Bossereau, a sixty-year-old Frenchman, who comes to America fired with zeal and with the support of the New Socialist Colonization Company to found a Socialistic commune on the frontier of North Texas in what is today the western part of metropolitan Dallas. Bossereau served as a delegate to the French Constitutional Assembly and was also a writer and editor in the thick of the French Revolution where the effort to overthrow the monarchy led to a blood bath at the guillotine. He is a paradox as Langly describes him. He has a fair complexion, a thin sensitive nose, and thin skin. Langly says, "In sum, he seemed tender to the minor pains and itches of existence, but this did not add up to the impression he made. One could not be in his presence without being aware of the force of his opinion; one could not look at him without being aware of a great mind working behind the high forehead" (First edition, 10). But he fails, as Martin Bucco notes, because he is "too innocent to realize his glorious plan" (309).

The setting in which the group founded the colony was far different in 1848 than it is today. At that time, this section of Texas was inhabited mostly by Indians. The few whites who lived in the region were the kind of social outcasts comfortable on the fringes of civilized culture.

The plot opens as the settlers' wagons and livestock approach the "broad shallow valley" where they are to found the ideal colony, one based on reason, brotherly love, and communal property. The pace of the action in the novel is slow and the development of the plot deliberate. Capps's accomplishment in this work is the careful chronicling of the founding, growth, and failure of the socialistic community of Uterica. He based his account on a similar effort made on what is now the western edge of Dallas, Texas, in 1855 in an area called La Reunion and another called Icaria, located in 1848 between present-day Fort Worth and Denton. In the novel Capps reveals his grasp of the socialistic commune ideal common in the 1840s and 1850s when the spirit of freedom and revolution were common in Europe and in America. The name Uterica is a combination of Utopia and America and emphasizes the idea of achieving a Utopian level of existence in North America (53).

Capps positions and develops his characters to represent several factors at work in the time—the high priest of Socialism, Jean Bossereau; his naive daughter, Jeanette; the feminist, Harriet Edwards; the totalitarian, Dr. Valentin; the perceptive Dr. Sockwell; the Unitarian, Brother Adams; the troublemaker, Deveraux; and the naive but resourceful tyro, Brother Langly, whose perceptions serve as the narrative mode of Capps's presentation. His objectivity is, as Richard W. Etulain notes (*Journal of the West* 657), so strongly developed that the novel suffers from the lack of enthusiasm of such a narrator as Huckleberry Finn, for example. The narrator is one of the socialists, and the leader of the group is a ministerial type selling foolishly optimistic socialism, not a gospel of doom and damnation as the frontier preacher usually does. Other figures of significance are the inept winemaker, Henri, and the York brothers, whose resourcefulness is rendered useless as the frontier first separates them and then causes Andrew to kill Jeanette.

The Indians in the novel, by Capps's own admission in the "Preface," represent a group that has adapted to the environment in which they live. Two kinds of Indians are present in the novel—the settled agricultural Indians and the mounted or "horse" Indians who mastered the wild horses of Spanish descent and radically changed their lifestyle to accommodate the horse. Knowledge and possession of the horse led to improved methods of travel and hunting as well as the shock tactic of mounted cavalry in warfare. Both groups have learned how to survive and even to prosper.

The Indians also represent in Capps's mind "the unknown, mysterious, even dangerous consequences that await thinkers who learn too much from each other and not enough about nature" (ix). The contrast between the Indian and the colonists in this regard is enormous. Like the sea fowl that rests comfortably on the rolling swells of the high seas, the Indians are comfortable in their world, existing in harmony with nature. The colonists, on the other hand, are like land birds over the threatening waves, frantically searching for a place to rest after having flown too far from the sanctuary of land without realizing their plight, until it is too late. The colonists lack the knowledge and skills to survive. Becoming involved in the trapping expedition, an activity that provided Sam Chance, for example, cash to develop his ranching operation, could have been the key to the survival of the colony. But their principles prohibit them and, thus, condemn them to failure.

Harriet Edwards, apparently the victim of an unhappy marriage, is intent on promoting other women into nontraditional roles in the community. Although inspired by lofty motives, she is totally impractical for this situation and eventually is defeated.

The long philosophical essays that Langly writes, the product of his efforts at lofty thought, are revealing. The basic irony that underlies the situation developed in the novel is unwittingly revealed in Langly's essay written upon the death of Jeanette. In his discussion of learning to play poker, a game not allowed in Uterica, he says it is "a fascinating game of chance, possibility, probability, these mixed with the personalities of fellow players, mingled with a few known certainties, stirred up with expectation" (252). The venture at Uterica runs strangely parallel; he is accurately discussing the gamble called life. He notes that there is no certainty of instructions in the game—poker or life—and one must depend on Lady Luck, always fickle, of course. Even at his best, Langly writes of man, "let him be taught by experience to play cautiously, and, sure enough, some bold coup will strike him on his blind innocent side; let him reply in kind to this new experience, and he has left the other flank exposed" (252). He then praises an old soldier who played with a group of men in the days when Langly was learning the game. He ponders the old soldier's skill: "I began to have the dubious but persistent thought that something more was involved than skillful mastery of the principles and the unpredictable, disinterested Lady." He waits his chance. "The opportunity came when he and I sat alone waiting for the other players, and I asked him straight out: 'What, in your opinion, is the secret of it?' He frowned at me as if my question were an unexpected insult and opened his mouth and said, 'Play to win'" (253). The failure of the colony seems based on Langly's weakness—playing, for sport or for principle, not to win. The colony is being built to prove a point, not to win an existence in a difficult environment. A man needs a lifetime of learning how to manipulate the unknowns in a gamble like farming. A rank amateur in that endeavor should not try. Langly, Bossereau, and all the other colonists learn that lesson the hard way.

Another facet of this kind of noble but destructive thinking is found in Bossereau's lectures to the group. When he should have spent time teaching them how to survive, he shows his lack of understanding by addressing such subjects as "Modern Women and the Socialist Society." His zeal and dream are admirable; his methods spell disaster for the colony.

In the preface he wrote for the 1988 Southern Methodist University Press reissue of the novel, Capps notes the problem faced by all Utopian societies. He says that Plato's *Republic* and More's *Utopia* "assume that human life can be well ordered by human reason." Then he notes the flaw of such notions: "No such proposal has solved the problem of whose reason shall be used and how leaders should be selected" (vii). He then elaborates on two particulars of his understanding of More's *Utopia:* "First, More sets his ideal society in the New World. Out there somewhere was virgin land, not tainted by the old problems of wealth and privilege and custom, a place where reasonable people of good will could start over. All America was the West at the time, and parts of it would remain the West for four hundred years." Capps continues:

> The second notable aspect of More's *Utopia* has to do with the education of those who are setting up the ideal society. People in the city would go out to the farms, More wrote, "to be instructed and taught by those who have been there a year already, and are therefore expert and skilled in the care and cultivation of the

> land. And they the next year shall teach the others." Such an attitude is citified intellectual arrogance; any country bumpkin knows that it takes a lifetime to understand the vagaries of weather and insects and stock breeding. (vii–viii)

Capps also reveals in his preface the range of his research on the subject. He comments on the existence of such communes in pre–Civil War America. Sixty-two, for example were west of the Mississippi between 1860 and 1919; and in pre–Civil War times, three quarters of such colonies were on the frontier of their day. American colonists gravitated to the frontier, and like those in *The Brothers of Uterica,* they were ill prepared to cope with and conquer the problems of settling an area where agricultural practices, native inhabitants, weather, and other such important matters were poorly understood.

One is reminded, as Capps notes, of other fictional accounts of such "colonies," such as Nathanial Hawthorne's *The Blithedale Romance,* and even darker ones, Aldous Huxley's *Brave New World* and George Orwell's *Nineteen Eighty-Four.* He then correctly notes that this material "has hardly been treated in fiction of the American West" (ix).

One reason for the absence of fictional treatment of this kind of activity is the lack of traditional "Western" action inherent in it. The novel is, as

Sonnichsen says in his "Afterword" to the Southern Methodist University Press edition, "a fresh and original work" (314)—but the work is so atypical in some ways from other novels about the region that it has been largely ignored. And understandably so. The label of "Western" has no bearing on this work, and readers still seem to demand at least some traditional action and conflict between frontier elements. True, this work has horses, cattle, sheep, guns, wagons, Indians, and other such ingredients expected of the Western, but these are saddle horses, not cow horses; milk cows and not stampeding herds of longhorns (even though longhorns do come through and "break out" the domesticated cattle and kill the herd bull); sheep that become the dietary mainstay; guns that are poorly handled; wagons that ferry building supplies and trade goods; and Indians who eventually overwhelm the colonists' will to exist and burn the village. Readers of traditional Westerns would not finish reading this one.

Perhaps most clearly in *The Brothers of Uterica,* of all his writing, Capps proves his intention to write what he wants to write. As Sonnichsen says in his "Afterword," Capps will not "prostitute himself for popularity" (311) or "pander to popular taste" (312). He broke away from any Western stereotypes in this book.

Nonetheless, C.W. Smith's praise of the book is

high: "The novel is remarkable not only for its strength of mind—the characters are all passionate devotees of their ideas and argue them eloquently—but also for Capps's ability to allow his character to be fallibly human first, and representative of ideas, second. The tension between practical needs and ideological concerns eventually puts a wedge in the solidarity the would-be colonists feel, but then individual selfishness in conflict with the general good puts an end to the grand experiment" (7).

The novel reflects in heroic proportion the failure of the colony—desertion by the colonists, lack of leadership and dedication to foolish idealism, the death of Jeanette Bossereau, the lack of understanding the pitfalls involved in farming on the edge of the rolling Plains, the danger of the Indians, and the lack of understanding of basic human motivation. The New England dreamers Ralph Waldo Emerson and Henry David Thoreau would have been at home in Uterica and would have seen no reason to be alarmed by its inevitable doom.

The Heirs of Franklin Woodstock

Another non-Western novel is *The Heirs of Franklin Woodstock,* Capps's most recent novel and his most mature work. It differs from his other novels in the contemporary setting and conflict, but like the others, it is an intense character study, this time of several modern individuals in conflict with each other in a ranch setting in West Texas. In this novel, Capps culminates his entire career for he includes ideas on a socialistic community somewhat like that in Uterica, ranching practices much like those he dealt with in *Sam Chance,* and even some Indian background such as he used in his Indian novels and histories.

The background of the sixty-six-year-old narrator, George Woodstock, the most fully developed character in the book, meshes neatly with much of Capps's own biographical detail. A machinist of considerable talent, Capps voices through Woodstock technical language, details of projects, and labor problems common in this business. George Woodstock also has in his background many of the details of Capps's early life—Capps's grandfather was a mustanger; Capps's father's middle name was Franklin; Capps himself graduated from high school in the late 1930s; he worked as a surveyor on a dam on the Red River, quit surveying to work for the U.S. Corp of Engineers in a salary dispute, and helped lay out new air fields at Grand Junction, Colorado, and Greenville, Texas; and he entered the U.S. Army Air Corps as an aviation cadet and became a navigator after schooling in California and Hondo, Texas. His service in the Pacific with the Seventh Air Force under Admiral Nimitz is accurate, as are his duty stations—Kwajalein and Guam—and the targets—Jaluit, Wake, Truk, Yap, Marcus, Chichi Jima, Haha Jima, and Iwo Jima. Capps's later career as a machinist, first at Chance-Vought and then at smaller shops, also is accurate.

Differences appear of course. His father was a cowboy and oil field worker, not a wealthy rancher, and died when Capps was a boy. Capps's one year at Texas Technological College does not parallel the life of George. After the war, however, Capps returned to college, an experience that George Woodstock has not chosen.

George's life is complicated by trying to get his new machine shop organized and built, but fortunately he has hired an outstanding machinist named Robert Fowler, on whom he comes to rely to run the shop and consider bids on jobs while George is away. He has also hired another named Wheeler, who misuses George's tools and machines and tries to organize the other workers in the shop into a union. George has to fire Wheeler, who proves completely inept and uncaring.

Parallel with these problems runs a series of frustrating confrontations with George's brothers and sisters about what to do with the 7,680-acre ranch now that Papa is definitely missing and is presumed dead. Walter, a graduate of the Harvard School of

Business and a stereotypical Texas business tycoon living in New York, wants to subdivide and develop the ranch into a playground for the rich. Walter hires accountants to examine the ranch's accounts, and he also hires a detective named Dobbs who chases weak leads all over the United States in search of the missing rancher whose health is far too fragile to allow the old man to survive such traveling. When Walter confronts the staff at the nursing home, he gets no more information than George did and is enraged and determined that through his business connections he will get some of the employees fired. He is unsuccessful in that regard; New York influence counts for little in remote West Texas.

Walter's attitude toward other people is represented in his question to George at the ranch when he unloads one of his bags from the car and asks—"Aren't you going to lock your car?" Walter trusts no one. He has lived in New York so long that he has lost contact with the rural folk and their ethics.

The business tycoon's deal is opposed by another twentieth-century mania—the religious retreat. Irma, George's younger sister, epitomizes the "born again" Southern Baptist believer of the radical right-wing persuasion that is threatening to split the Southern Baptist Convention in the late 1980s. She is certain that Papa is "born again" despite

George's lack of conviction on that notion and is pushing for the ranch to become a haven for Christians. The new center, to be called Noah's Ark, would be available only to members fleeing from the death and destruction of the atomic bomb when it is inevitably dropped, as Irma and her evangelist son, Wilbur, are sure that it will be. At the time of the disaster, the members will gather at the retreat, arm themselves, and kill nonmembers who try to enter the Christian haven. Irma and Wilbur are convinced that careful attention will have to be given to having on the ranch various seeds for planting crops as well as pairs of animals for breeding, which would, in their opinion, have to include camels. Wilbur, who has left his pulpit ministry to become an evangelist, intends to be the president of the organization and has agreed to serve for a salary of only sixty thousand dollars a year, not the one hundred thousand dollars a year that his mother feels he deserves. The center will have a powerful radio station that, when the crisis comes, will broadcast the message that "the Ark is ready to float," thereby encouraging members who are having a difficult time getting to the sanctuary because of an anarchist society gone crazy from fear. Wilbur manages to get an invitation to speak at the local Baptist church while visiting the ranch with his mother, who is determined to support Wilbur in any way possible, a pattern she is already following by providing financing for her son.

Clarence, George's younger brother, a college English professor in California, comes with his son, Frank, to the ranch when school is out. Their plan for the property is to develop an oil company to drill wells on the ranch and on surrounding areas that they will lease. By forming the company, the heirs will get all the money from the wells, not just the landowner's one-eighth share. Anyone familiar with the search for oil deposits realizes the fallacy of Clarence and Frank's assumption; the oil business is a gamble with very unfavorable odds against success.

George has his own plan, but not for the ranch. Papa had promised him one hundred thousand dollars to buy equipment for a model machine shop George wants to build. The plan is elaborate. George wants to develop a shop run by five able co-owners who also work in the operation to oversee the work of others. In this way, the co-owners would eliminate various administrative jobs, and the operation would be far more efficient and profitable than most of its kind. George has no witnesses to the promise of the money, which was to be supplied when George needed it. Now that his father is missing and presumed dead, however, George sees little hope in getting the money other than through the settlement of the estate.

Clara, the "ding-bat" of the family, has no plan except to spoil her grandchildren, much to the distress of her daughter-in-law.

The wild schemes of Walter, Irma, and Clarence contrast sharply with the ideas of Izzy and Johnny, thought by other family members to be only a Mexican cook and her son who live at the ranch. These two want the place to remain the ranch they love and to honor the memory of the man they loved. Izzy is a fecund Earth Mother figure, chosen by a band of Indians to be their spiritual guide in a question over how to fund part of their transition into modern life, a move that Papa agrees to fund with a forty thousand dollar check. Izzy cooks, cleans house, makes beds, and in every way she can takes care of the Woodstock clan. She has canned and frozen so much food from her garden that she must give it to local needy people. She then begins once again to plant a large garden in order to preserve additional food. Her son Johnny, the ranch manager, is a fine cowman and organizer who stayed to work with Papa and made the old man's dreams for the ranch come true. He is the kind of help Papa wanted and needed, unlike the first generation of Woodstock children, who have paid little attention to their father over the years. In fact, they have no good photographs of him to furnish the detective who is trying to find their father.

Franklin Woodstock never appears in the novel, but he is well developed through inference. He loves his children and their offspring, despite failings such as Homer's mental incompetence and Walter's aggressiveness. Franklin will, for example, bequeath to his great-granddaughter, Annie, the flowers and insects on the ranch and take time to do so in a written document, which he updates after his escape from the nursing home. He is an astute stockman and a rancher in the frontier tradition, a Sam Chance in modern times, who, by matching the strengths and weaknesses of the ranch, has built up a herd of two hundred heifers. He is a closet poet, who leaves behind evidence of his talent, and a humanitarian toward minority groups for he pays forty thousand dollars to the Indians on a nod of Izzy's head. He also has a sense of humor, especially in the way he leaves the heirs to sort things out after his death intestate. The surprise that Izzy actually is his wife and Johnny is his son is certainly not humorous to Walter and the others, but George has realized a need for Izzy and Johnny to have part of the place to ranch. Papa did not quit living when his children by his first wife left to pursue their own fortunes. He continued running the ranch until his health required that he be put into a nursing home. Then he escaped from the nursing home, came to the ranch, modified his will to provide for Annie, and then probably caused part of Dead Cowbones Bluff to cave in on him, burying him on the piece of land he loved.

Obviously, the family is as fragmented as many modern families are. The children do not realize that after their mother died in middle age and the children had left home, Papa started life anew with a new wife and fathered a son who remained on the land to help him ranch it.

Much like Benjy Compson in William Faulkner's *The Sound and the Fury,* Homer is a perceptive half-wit. Clarence, the literary scholar, calls his great nephew "an idiot-savant. He has his wires crossed in his head so that his balance is bad and things sometimes seem to be upside down. Also it is a motor function disorder, but they have found people who have made an impression like Homer does, and yet are especially competent in some things. They surprise people" (177). Homer does indeed surprise everyone when he proves Johnny's birthright by what Homer calls "my papers"—Papa and Izzy's marriage license and Johnny's birth certificate showing Papa as his father.

Johnny is well aware of his rights and of his expectations. He has accepted Papa's death without betraying it to outsiders, but purchasing a new Jeep reveals his knowledge that he will receive money from the settlement of the estate. It is important to note that he buys a vehicle adapted to the ranch, not a fast town car. The difference between Papa's oldest by his first wife and the first-born of his second is evident when Johnny leaves the key in the Jeep in case someone wants to use it.

Johnny has quit searching the ranch for Papa because he knows the truth of his death. He goes with the two children and George to Dead Cowbones Bluff to say goodbye to Papa. Annie lets slip just enough information to let the reader know the truth, which supports George's speculations. Capps cleverly lets one of the major pieces of the puzzle come from the natural scientist from Harvard, who notes that part of the bluff at the bone site collapsed not long after Papa disappeared. Papa undoubtedly got his business taken care of and then died in peace.

One other detail about the death comes in a comment by Clarence on a work by a writer named "Capp" in which an Indian "threw himself away," an incident found in *A Woman of the People*. Thus, Capps plants the notion that Papa committed suicide when he saw that his life was over. He is therefore identified with the primitive independence of frontier people. Just as he was sympathetic with Izzy's role as Earth Mother to the band of Indians, Papa chose his own method of departing, one he saw as honorable, as opposed to dying in the nursing home where nurses took away his dignity and fed him foods that he detested. By being buried at Dead Cowbones Bluff, his bones may one day wash out on the plains, and he will join the continuum of time along with other relics of the past.

Capps uses the events to deal in some detail with the social and cultural phenomenon of the nursing home as the final step before the grave for old people. Variously dressed in street clothes and bed clothes, the residents of the local facility—more women than men—are mostly staring into space. One woman nods; another shakes her head back and forth in a continuous negation of life. All have no zest for life and seem to be waiting for death. Capps speculates about their lives, their hopes, their dreams—all now passed and actually dead. What Capps highlights is the lack of dignity for residents in a nursing home. As one of the nurses points out, the routine is mechanical. On certain days, nurses chart various details of the residents' lives. One time a nurse asked Papa to go to the bathroom in a bedpan so the nurses could weigh the result; instead, he spit tobacco juice in the bedpan and told the nurse to weigh that. The diet is carefully controlled, so much so that the nurse who is furnishing the special blended broiled steak and mushroom soup and beer for Papa is forced to resign. The crucial charge against the culture, however, is that the younger members of a family, busy with lives and careers and unwilling to give the attention needed, turn old people over to this mechanized process but become disturbed when treatment is not personalized. When, for example, elderly patients, who may be very difficult to control, must be tied to a wheelchair to ensure that they do not try to walk and perhaps fall and injure themselves, the families are horrified to see the loved ones restrained. But they are quick to respond, often with a threat of a lawsuit, if elderly patients are injured when not supervised. The quality of help at minimum wage to do this kind of work is questionable. The staff members care for the patients, even cry when they die, but the profit margin is a driving force in the number and quality of staff.

This latest of Capps's works may be his best. In technique, it is superior to most of the others, which have passages where Capps rushes the action. The characterizations here are representative of Capps's other books, and especially strong is George, who parallels Sam Chance and Charley Blankenship, two of Capps's most memorable characters. In pace and style, the novel flows smoothly and has artistic flair without being showy. This is good, solid fiction at its best. Capps's canon is enhanced by this late addition.

The six novels that deal with the Anglo experience in the West are diverse in form and in the period used as the setting. For subject matter, Capps has dealt with law and order and the cattle kingdom, but he has also included trapping, buffalo hunting, and other activities in the West as well as the failed effort of a socialistic commune. He closes his career to date with a contemporary novel, which is not really a Western at all in the traditional sense. His contribution to literary art in the Western genre is considerable, but his total output has not been restricted to the Anglo experience, as the next chapter reveals.

3

THE INDIAN NOVELS

Capps has a lasting interest in the Indian of the American West. His perceptive grasp of and interest in Indians led to his writing three novels dealing with these native Americans in the western United States from the 1830s to the turn of the century. From 1949 to 1951, while living and teaching at the college in Tahlequah, Oklahoma, Capps became familiar with a culture descended from many famous old warriors and chiefs, but the individuals he met were everyday people, mostly college students striving to find their way in the white man's world, a trying situation that no doubt intrigued him. These three novels—*Woman Chief* (1979), *A Woman of the People* (1966), and *The White Man's Road* (1969)—present a perceptive survey of the Indians of the American West during the decades that saw their culture at its height before it was crushed by the westward-moving Anglos.

In the first two of these novels, Capps has made

use of the experience of the mounted or horse Indians on the western Plains. As Robert A. Roripaugh points out, most of the interpretative fiction dealing with the Indians of the West has concerned "agricultural tribes" (65), particularly Navajos and other pueblo dwellers in such works as Frank Waters' *The Man Who Killed the Deer,* Oliver LaFarge's *Laughing Boy,* and later Leslie Silko's *Ceremony* and the numerous unconventional Navajo detective novels of Tony Hillerman. Certainly N. Scott Momaday's modern Indians portrayed in *The House Made of Dawn* are not the Kiowas when they rode the open plains. The life and activities of the nomadic, warlike tribes have been more easily adapted to the traditional action Western with the hordes of screaming Indians attacking settlers and chasing or being chased by cavalry soldiers.

Capps depicts the warlike Plains Indians at a time when they were caught in the grip of time, place, and circumstance that demanded the best leadership to avoid extinction. He is interested in the relationships and conflicts of various Indian tribes as well as in the often-depicted conflict between Indians and whites. Like any other group of people, the Indians warred among themselves, counting coup, taking lives for revenge, and plundering goods in order to live. In some ways, the "primitive" Indians differed little from European tribes of an earlier day.

Woman Chief

Woman Chief is a medium-length novel dealing with conflict among Indians. Set in the early to mid-1880s, the novel tells of a legendary woman chief of the Crow Indians on the Yellowstone River in that part of the West that is now Wyoming and North and South Dakota. Capps indicates in his introductory note that the real person on whom the character is based lived "a century and a half ago" (First edition, viii), before Anglo encroachment became a factor in the Indians' lives. In this novel, Capps has done what those critical of his approach in *The Warren Wagontrain Raid* wanted done—he has fictionalized from his sources without notes other than to cite Edwin Thompson Denig, an early ethnologist who recorded the story of Woman Chief, as well as Rudolph Kurz, an explorer in the region, and later "scholars" such as Frank Linderman and John Ewers, all able commentators on the Crow Indians.

The novel is a *bildungsroman* dealing with the life of the woman through the stages indicated by her names—Slave Girl, Horse Tender, and Woman Chief; but she is also known by other names—Sweet

Thunder Woman and Absaroki Amazon. The plot is developed in a straightforward fashion with no distracting flashbacks or other narrative ploys. The story begins with a raid by Crow Indians from High Owl's band led by Elk Head on a village of Atsinas, derogatorily called Hairy Noses or Big Bellies. Antelope Man, one of the raiders, is determined to kidnap a male child to replace his only son, who had drowned in the flood-swollen and ice-choked Yellowstone River. The raid is a success, with many horses and much plunder taken. But Antelope Man by mistake captures a ten-year-old girl, "a wild-cat" whose fierce temperament impresses the raiders, who nonetheless laugh loudly at Antelope Man's blunder.

The girl is immediately dedicated to pleasing her new "father," for she was orphaned by a smallpox outbreak and is pleased to have family ties, regardless of how tenuous they are. She early demonstrates talents associated with men—vigilance when on watch, the skill to ride and break horses, and the ability to handle weapons. Despite these talents—perhaps because of them—her effort to gain acceptance as an equal in Antelope Man's family is long and painful. Broken Ice, the mother-in-law, and See Dead Bull, the first wife, are offended that Antelope Man has brought a girl home rather than a boy. Pea Finder, Antelope Man's aunt, and Birdy, the second of Antelope Man's wives and sister to See Dead Bull, are less opposed to the young girl, although they sometimes strike her.

From her first day in Antelope Man's household, Slave Girl tries to fit in by finding a place to sleep and a time to eat that do not conflict with other members of the family. But she hits a fierce dog that barks at her as she is going to the water hole and "thus she did on her first morning in the camp of her adopted people begin to learn and to assert herself in a humble way" (21) and "make for herself a niche, a place to exist, somewhere between the dogs and the human beings" (22).

By the end of the first year with High Owl's band of Crows, she is spending at least half her time tending horses despite Broken Ice and See Dead Bull's resentment at Antelope Man's letting her do so. Now called Horse Tender, she becomes more and more adept at riding horses. She befriends Ride Away, a Crow boy her own age. They talk, race their horses, and eat lunch together. Later, they become lovers.

Horse Tender's fascination for weapons is further developed when Antelope Man cuts a bundle of serviceberry bush sprouts for arrows, bundles them with a wet rawhide thong, and hangs them beneath the smoke hole of the tepee to cure. Horse Tender prepares a second bundle, an act that angers See Dead Bull, who throws the bundle into the fire, but

Antelope Man retrieves it and compliments his young "daughter" for her able work. See Dead Bull's jealousy of the girl is obvious. She wants a slave to do the menial work and is angered when her husband defends the girl and lets her take the place of her dead son.

Horse Tender proves an adeptness with weapons that exceeds her years. For example, she understands arrow flight time as it affects accuracy and the strategy of the meat-stealing game, which the young men in the village play in order to learn the skills of thievery, considered important in the development of Crow warriors. She realizes that if one group were to start a diversion, others could steal whatever they wanted on the other side of the camp. As she tries to explain these ideas, Ride Away cannot understand her comments related to strategy. She becomes frustrated, and he is intimidated by her prowess.

One of the unusual characters in the story is a trader named Chicago, who is married to a Crow woman by whom he has fathered two children. He befriends the young captive girl and is impressed with her command of various languages—Absaroka, Blackfoot, Atsina, Crow, Spanish, and even a vague understanding of French and some English words. He offers her advice throughout the story and serves as a sounding board for some of her ideas.

One of the sacred ceremonies of the tribe is to broil a bear's heart and feed portions of it to the young men so that they may symbolically share the bravery of the bear. Since she is a female, Horse Tender is not allowed to participate in this ceremony, but she desires the experience. In order to have a part in this ritual, she kills a huge grizzly bear, roasts the heart, and eats it, a "ceremony" intruded upon by Chicago, who warns her "Quit pushing yourself and fighting yourself. . . . Quit it, I tell you!" (98). But she ignores his warning and becomes a great hunter. She learns with Ride Away how to tire an antelope by having the two of them successively chase it on horseback and then kill it up close with her moderate-strength bow, which is not strong enough for killing shots from a long distance. She kills squirrels by herself, a task more easily done by two because a squirrel will usually hide on the other side of a tree and elude a single hunter. She also kills ducks and other small game. Later, she persuades Antelope Man to bring her a *bois d'arc* bow when he goes on a trading trip to the south. When he departs, he leaves Horse Tender in charge of his weapons and the horses. When she receives the crude *bois d'arc* bow on his return, she scrapes and shapes the rough wood to make it beautiful and powerful. Her skill with it becomes legendary as she takes large game and slays enemies with her arrows. The weapon is rumored to be magical.

Horse Tender has contradictory desires. Her masculine drives cause her constantly to want to know more about the male society. She even asks Ride Away what men talk about in the sweat lodges. He tells her little but does mention personal medicine. She wonders if thunder can be a source of personal medicine, for she prays to the thunder. Her female side also causes her to want to be courted, and she demands to have a child, but, as Chicago tells her, in order to become pregnant she must quit riding horseback every day. She refuses to stop her riding and seeks a magic way of having a child by visiting a sacred spot on Arrow Creek, a place that Pea Finder tells her children can be requested. Her quest is unsuccessful.

Honor in war comes to her. For example, the men of Streaked Hair, a war chief of a band of enemy Sioux, attack the nearby Crow village of Chickadee. Horse Tender leads in helping survivors get to shelter on the cold spring night. She tearfully buries a dead baby for the band in a kind of catharsis for the child she had long wanted but never had. A band from High Owl's village under the leadership of a chief named Rainy goes to avenge the fallen Crows. With this action, the real legend of Woman Chief begins: although forbidden to ride with the warriors, she goes anyway, keeping out of sight of the Crow warriors, killing many of the enemy, and scalping the fierce Streaked Hair. Some of the Indians on the raid see another person but think it is a spirit sent by *Napa,* a god helper, and think it is a bad sign (120).

When peace efforts come to the area, the Crows decide to go to a Great Conference. Woman Chief first talks against the meeting but later changes her mind, and with good reason, for by this time she has adopted two children, a boy and a girl who had been orphaned. They become the children she could never bear, and she gives them the names that she had long cherished—Brave Rider and Pink Morning. This situation provides a touch of domesticity lacking before, as if her frustration with not having a family is taken out in the ways of war, in slaughtering her enemies.

After leading at the conference, the Crows go to their homeland, now assured by treaty. Woman Chief then gives herself to the cause of peace. Against all advice, she takes five warriors to make a peace venture to the Atsinas, her own people. She gives away her best possession and rides off, only to be shot down with her party by a group of the Atsinas when they realize who she is. Apparently, she knows that she is going to be killed, but, as she says, "I think it is important that we made the gesture of trust and friendship" (224). Capps says, "Legend would imply that in some certain fullness of time she was called back to where she came from" (226). The story ends with her death among the tall grasses of the prairie over which she rode. No mention is made of Woman Chief's grave or even if the remains of her and the five warriors are retrieved. Antelope Man is now old, but he has a vision about the child he captured who turned into a great chief of his band.

The notion of a woman leader of a band of Plains Indians, although not commonplace, is not unknown. The Apaches, for example, sometimes let women ride and fight alongside their warrior husbands. Lozen, the sister of the famous Apache chief Victorio, was known as the Woman Warrior. A veteran of raids with Geronimo and Victorio, she also helped in the negotiations between the Apaches and the American military officers in ending Apache depredations in the southwestern United States and Mexico. In her account of the exploits of this Indian, historian Eve Ball records from one of her informants a description of Lozen, which parallels Capps's depiction of Woman Chief: "I knew of no other woman bidden to the council, but that was because no other had the skill as a warrior that Lozen did. She could ride, shoot, and fight like a man; and I think she had more ability in planning military strategy than did Victorio. At that time I speak of, she had not married, she went on the warpath with the men, which no woman other than the wives of warriors was permitted to do; and she was held in the greatest respect by them, much as though she were a holy person" (21).

Other instances exist as well. Ralph Smith records an example among Comanches, when Grandma Sol, known as the "generaless of the Comanches" as well as "prophetess" and "the she wolf of the Southern Comanches" led her sons and others on years of raiding and plundering in Texas and Mexico before she was killed in a raid by Mexicans (25–26). Richardson describes another—the widow of a great Penateka Chief, Santa Anna, who was "one of the best hunters in the tribe" (216).

A fictionalized version of this notion is found in Frederick Manfred's *Manly-Hearted Woman*. Manfred, who writes about the Sioux of the northern Plains, depicts the exploits of a woman who is magically, perhaps mystically, transformed into a "manly-hearted woman" and assumes many of the traits of a warrior, even to the point of no longer wanting to engage in practices, sexual and other, associated with women. Later, she is demystified and resumes her role as a woman when a charm credited with causing her change disappears.

Capps's use of Edwin Thompson Denig's account is remarkably accurate for the most part, with few variations between the historical and fictional accounts. Denig's treatise, titled *Of the Crow Nation* and published by the Bureau of American Ethnology in Washington, D.C., in 1953, is apparently derived from first-hand knowledge, for he says that he knew Woman Chief "from a personal acquaintance of twelve years" (65). The masculine and warring tendencies, the taking of scalps and horses from the enemy, the remaining unmarried—all are closely followed by Capps, as are the incidents of her killing the three Blackfeet at the fort and the circumstances of her death and the singing of songs about her.

Capps's fictionalizing is well done within the framework of the historical account. The variations do not detract from the authenticity of the work and add continuity and focus to the story. The characterizations and details in the novel make it a far more impressive and personal experience for the reader than Denig's roughly four pages of narrative could possibly do. For instance, the historical account indicates that many songs were sung to recount the exploits of Woman Chief. Capps creates these songs, none of which are included in Denig's historical account. Also, the folk element in the story is strong, for Capps adds to the legend's details, which were more than likely subject to universalization of the motifs involved in the concept of the hero, especially of an Amazon. He also incorporates many details of

Indian life, including breaking horses, making and repairing weapons, waging war, building fires and sharing them with neighbors, and engaging in domestic routine such as tanning hides and getting water for personal use in the lodges. Finally, Capps humanizes his heroine by injecting comments on her fears (of being beaten as a child), her sorrows (at losing the man she loved), her victories (over the threatening dogs as well as over men), her outbursts of anger (at Ride Away and others), her ability to help the other women of the tribe, her desire to have a father and mother figure, and her desire to have children, whom she adopts.

The novel is not one of Capps's best, but the development of a female character is sensitively done. Although Capps refuses to write any explicitly sexual material, that part of Woman Chief's life is not ignored. It receives the same degree of attention given to her skills in hunting and riding and in domestic and diplomatic affairs. The approach is objective and the history fairly represented, as it is in other Capps novels about Native Americans.

A Woman of the People

One of Capps's best novels is *A Woman of the People,* a Book-of-the-Month Club selection in 1966. This fictionalized Indian captivity narrative depicts the events in the life of Helen Morrison and her sister, Katy. At the time of their capture in 1854, Helen is nine years old and Katy is five. For the setting of this novel, Capps uses a region he knows well, the western part of Texas and Oklahoma. The Indians roamed this area, where Capps grew up, as well as that near Lubbock, where he first attended college on the Llano Estacado. The Comanches shared this large region, teeming with buffalo and other game, with the Kiowas and jealously defended it against the enemy Tonkawas and various bands of Apaches and later the whites.

Capps uses a familiar model as the basis of the historical element in the book. Helen Morrison's capture and assimilation into Comanche life parallel in many ways the experience of Cynthia Ann Parker, a nine-year-old girl kidnapped by Comanche Indians from Fort Parker on the Navasota River in Limestone County, Texas, in May of 1836. Cynthia Ann was taken along with two women, Elizabeth Kellogg and Rachel Plummer, as well as Plummer's fifteen-month old son, James, and six-year-old John Parker, Cynthia Ann's brother. The Comanche band escaped toward the Trinity River, the area that Capps uses as the setting of his story. Cynthia Ann was able to make the transition into Indian life and later married Peta Nocona, an important warrior who eventually led the band to which he belonged.

Cynthia Ann bore children by him, the most famous of whom was Quanah, recognized as the most knowledgeable and powerful chief of the Comanches at the time of their surrender at Fort Sill. Capps moved his narrative forward in time so that Helen's, or Tehanita's, relationship with the Indians coincides with the Mutsani band's surrender to reservation life. This parallel to Cynthia Ann Parker's experience is not the only possible historical parallel. The Millie Durgan story, which Capps includes in *The Warren Wagontrain Raid,* offers some parallels as well.

Capps avoids part of the sequence of events that can be anticipated for Tehanita by ending the novel at the time the Indians ride onto the reservation. Once the whites discover that Tehanita is actually a white woman, she may well be forced to return to Anglo life. The plight of a woman "rescued" from Indian captivity was not always a fortunate one, as T.R. Fehrenbach indicates: "'The frontier's puritanical views and rigid racial and sexual shibboleths made it impossible for such unfortunate women to be accepted gracefully back into their communities. . . . When they could, such women left the frontier and all old associations forever" (289). Cynthia Ann Parker did not wish to return to her white relations, but she was forced to make a transition beyond her power. She soon sickened and died.

The style of *A Woman of the People* is typical of Capps's best work—carefully restrained prose that Lee calls in his "Afterword" to the 1985 edition "simple and unadorned" (247) and that Roripaugh calls "sparse, uncomplicated" (40), with a linear plot containing little deviation from the central focus on the developing character of Helen Morrison into Tehanita, the Comanche wife of Burning Hand and the mother of his son. The dialogue is plausibly natural, once the Pidgin English of Talking Woman is left behind early in the plot when she speaks the English she has learned from whites in order to communicate with Helen. The action, though dramatic, is not sensationally depicted. The bloodshed and horror that could have been a major focus is downplayed, with the exception of the torture of the Tonkawa. The horror of rape by enemy Indians and soldiers is omitted from the direct relating in the narrative. Lee's statement concerning the themes of the captivity narrative and the "cultural equality" points out the richness of the novel in its concerns for character and culture (1985 edition, 245).

Capps uses a curious situation to point to the climax of the novel and the conclusion of the Comanches' old way of life. When Burning Hand is at Medicine Mounds seeking his medicine, he is disappointed that Tehanita interrupts his vigil. He says, "A mist had come before my eyes, and that is a good sign. It means one might have a vision. Then what happens? You come along and spoil it!" (80). Without realizing it, Burning Hand has received a powerful vision—Tehanita. She is the one to lead him in the way the personal medicine is supposed to lead an Indian who has purified himself and waited to receive such a gift. It is Tehanita who counsels him in his adult years, bears him the son named Little Hunter, and otherwise prepares him to lead his people out of the Stone Age and into the present. The little girl who was almost killed because she was thought to be too old to assimilate into the tribe and too young to be a slave becomes the medium through which the salvation of the tribe is worked out.

Burning Hand, despite the belief that he has never received his personal medicine, becomes the Chief and tries to decide on the best plan for the band. One day Tehanita sees him studying a revolver. He sees its complexity, realizes that the technology of the whites surpasses that of the Comanche, and understands the impact of that knowledge. He asks her, since she "used to be white," if she remembers anything about the whites. She must answer no. He decides he must study the whites and rides eastward. She follows, trying to remain out of view. Finally, she approaches him as he watches a white man's house. She confesses her old plan to return to the white culture but admits that she cannot without her son, her sister's child, and her husband. The two steal a large white sheet from the clothesline of the white family and later use it as a flag of truce as they ride in to surrender at Fort Sill. Instead of looking forward to being released from her Indian captivity, she rides proudly on her horse as she follows her husband. She tells her young son, "Sit up proudly and straight. . . . See your father, how he sits" (242). A brilliant chapter in Comanche life comes to a close as the novel ends.

In his "Afterword" to this novel, Lee expresses some cogent views on what Capps chose *not* to do with the novel. He notes that the novel is not the typical hysterical horror story of a young female captured by Indians because, he says, Capps avoids what Richard Slotkin labels "the salvation-through-affliction theme so dear to the hearts of the New England Puritans," who made morality pieces of the stories and capitalized on the "literary and social consequences of the mythology implicit in the captivity narratives" (244, quoting Slotkin). As Lee notes, Capps depicts the "captive beginning to see values in the culture of the captors" (244). Here, a crucial difference appears—Helen "is unlike most of the heroes and heroines of captivity literature in that she is never freed, she never tells her story to the 'outside.' Instead of seeing her return to 'civilization' to proclaim her ardors and teach the lessons that she learned, we see her blend completely into the culture of the captors. She is not regenerated through suffering but is civilized by the humanity of the Indians" (244–45). Capps's use of a nine-year-old narrator also saves him from depicting the typical brutal treatment accorded women who were captured by Indians.

Capps shows his knowledge of the various bands of Comanches. All of the divisions he mentions (47) can be confirmed in the best books on the subject: Wallace and Hoebel's *The Comanches: Lords of the South Plains,* which he acknowledges using, and Fehrenbach's *Comanches: The Destruction of a People.* One can rest comfortably knowing that Capps's use of history is carefully researched and accurately depicted. It is interesting to note, however, that the Mutsanis—called the Undercut Bank Indians because they liked to camp "underneath an overhanging cliff" (Wallace and Hoebel 30)—were annihilated in a battle with Mexicans around 1845. Helen's abduction occurs in 1854. Capps has used accurate names of tribes, but he has improvised on history, giving new life to a band annihilated earlier.

One historical fact that Capps includes is the warning given to the Mutsanis that soldiers will converge on them from every direction. Fehrenbach recounts that in 1874, the situation was as Capps describes it: "MacKenzie marched from Fort Concho with the 4th

Cavalry and supporting infantry, the 'Southern column'—about six hundred men with thirty scouts. Colonel Nelson A. Miles moved west from Fort Leavenworth toward the Arkansas. Lieutenant Colonel Davidson operated out of Sill, Buell along the Red River, and William Price's column moved into *Comancheria* from New Mexico. The Comanches and Kiowas were to be surrounded and ground down between these converging forces" (539). Part of the battle resulting from this action was the attack on the Indians at Palo Duro Canyon, the raid in which Come Home Early is killed and the horse herd slaughtered. The actual raid was led by Col. Ranald MacKenzie on the morning of September 27, 1874. The Indians' secret wintering place in Palo Duro Canyon had been unknown to Anglos before this time, but MacKenzie had intercepted Comanchero Jose Tafoya and forced out of him—by stretching him on a wagon wheel—the trader's plan to go to Palo Duro to trade with the Indians. MacKenzie's scouts found the canyon and a means of descent just at dawn on the day of the battle. The soldiers burned the goods and food supplies and destroyed a thousand of the Indians' horses. This blow virtually ended the ability of Plains Indians to exist in the old way because the buffalo were too scarce to resupply the Indians with meat and skins, even if the weather had been good enough and the Indians had had their horses for hunting. Capps uses the historically accurate battle to end the hopes of the Mutsani band to continue to live in the wild just as was actually the case with many bands of the Plains Indians, particularly the Kwahadi band led by Cynthia Ann Parker's son, Quanah.

The book represents one of Capps's best efforts to weave history into the fabric of a novel. He is not subject to the criticism here that has been brought against *The Warren Wagontrain Raid,* in which he heavily fictionalized history. Instead, history serves as a supporting fabric for the tapestry of the novel.

Capps's grasp of the geography of the area used in the novel is as detailed and accurate as his use of history is. In a letter to this author on February 27, 1989, Capps recounts that he was a frequent traveler of the region "from the Little Bighorn to Horsehead Crossing on the Pecos." He also collected maps from government agencies, "some showing great detail." His explanation of some of the landmarks include the following: He admits to fictionalizing the small mesa that Tehanita tried to remember as a guide to lead her back to the world of the whites, but Goodwater and Badwater Creeks are his "surmise" of North Croton Creek in southern King County near Guthrie and the Salt Croton in northern Stonewall County. The Haystack Mountain is in southern King County, and the Double Mountains stand near Aspermont. The buffalo hunt taken from the camp on Goodwater Creek would have occurred along the Brazos River. The River of Tongues in the novel is now the Pease River in northern Texas, a stream that flows into the Red River northwest of Wichita Falls. The Wild River is the Cimarron, and Medicine Mounds are located in Hardeman County not far from present-day Quanah, Texas. The Springs of the People, once called Comanche Springs, is now called Big Spring, the site of a significant town in West Texas on Interstate 20. Arrowpoint River is a name the Indians applied to the Arkansas River. The Sandhills in which the Indians spent a summer are the famous sandhills near Monahans. The West Fork of the Trinity River along which the Morrison farm is located actually runs through present-day Tarrant, Wise, Jack, and Archer Counties of North Texas. And Yellow House Canyon is located in southeast Lubbock County.

The strong use of folklore in the novel includes Comanche myth, legend, and lore, as well as foodways and folk medicine. Myths include such stories as a river begun by a woman who cried, the source of the first buffalo, and the origin of horses (189). Legends and oral history of the tribe include the battle that the Comanches won by keeping their bow strings dry under their arms while those of their enemy became wet in the rain and did not operate efficiently. Stories also include those related to the

Spanish conquistadors and travel into a land where the birds "had brilliant feathers and little men danced in trees" (188), obviously Central America. Other lore includes the crawling snake sign for the Comanches, storytellers' narrative techniques, and the names for the seasons—for instance, Moon of the Thin Ice, Moon of the Howling Wind, and Moon of Babies Crying for Food. Folklore elements include methods of breaking horses, similar to those seen in *Woman Chief*, as well as the principal women of the lodge taking care of the warrior's weapons (40) and women occasionally traveling with their husbands on raids, as Sunflower does with Little Wild Horse when the two are killed.

Capps's emphasis on gathering and preparing foods is constant, as it was in the life of the Indians. Capps impresses the reader with the fact that the most important food element in the Indians' life was the buffalo. He details the methods of making jerky—preparing thin strips to dry on tree limbs or racks—and then making pemmican by combining layers of pounded jerky, dried nuts, and fruit, all covered with rendered tallow. He also includes the technique of hunting in a surround—when the mounted braves surround the herd and force it into a circle until a sufficient number of animals are killed—as well as methods of cooking in pots and skins lowered into a depression in the ground with hot rocks added, causing the ingredients of the makeshift pot to boil. He is also careful to mention the pounding holes in rocks, where various foods are pulverized, as well as the use of mesquite bean meal, prickly pear apples, sunflower seeds, and the ever-popular strips of raw buffalo liver laced with salty gall (65).

Methods of making and modifying tepees, the nature of lodge poles, the use of gear, packing and moving of the village, courtship and marriage customs, pipe smoking, and ritualistic dancing are all described in the novel. He also includes the superstition of the Comanches forced to eat dogs who constantly look behind them to see if evil spirits are pursuing them; he relates the proverb, "He who eats his horses lays up famine for the future" (62); and he even mentions Indian games such as kickball.

He is particularly aware of folk medicine in Spotting Dog's treatment of the wounded Ute Killer (197–98) as well as the actual treatments applied to the wounds by Talking Woman and the other women. He pays careful attention to funeral practices, especially in the method by which Ute Killer is buried (198–99) and the hasty method of burying in trees the Indians killed in the raid, a practice the Indians sometimes used, as Wallace and Hoebel indicate (149–50). Capps is a superb novelist and historian, but he is also a knowledgeable folklorist.

Critics have praised the book. Speck's estimate is worth quoting: "Capps has not told just another thrilling tale of Indian capture; rather, he has used that format to show something of Indian culture and to show the coming of the white man from the point of view of the Indian, who was as mystified by the white man's actions as any white man was by the Indian's" (*Benjamin Capps* 31). Roripaugh praises Capps for avoiding the "Western formula and myth" as well as the "inaccurate stereotype of the Indians." He shows that although the Indians are capable of cruelty, they also are "endowed with varying degrees of pride, humor, ambition, affection, and vanity" (66). Brian Garfield also praises Capps for portraying "the white man as the red man saw him: a vague, unrealized figure whose actions (fighting a Civil War, making incomprehensible treaties, slaughtering an entire tribe's horse-herd to force the tribe to come to the reservation) made no sense" (40).

Despite an overall favorable review, Roripaugh still faults Capps's characterizations. He says that Tehanita "remains somewhat one dimensional" and many of the Indians "seem to have been created from the outside without being made fully convincing as far as their inner development and individuality are concerned" (66). He concludes his review, however, by saying that "the novel is exceedingly honest, low keyed but moving, and refreshing in its portrayal of the century-back world of the Plains Indian. *A Woman of the People* deserves attention, and hopefully it, like Mr. Capps's two earlier novels, may reinforce the current uncertain trend toward higher literary standards in regional historical fiction" (66).

As he did in *Woman Chief,* Capps writes *A Woman of the People* from the viewpoint of a woman. By using the third person for his descriptions in extensive dialogue, Capps avoids the necessity of registering the many female perceptions on life from that point of view. He does not deal with emotional issues of love and jealousy, nor with woman as a plaything of men. He handles the story objectively and with great humanness and a sincere concern for emotion felt from loss, joy, fear, and hate—emotions common to men and women in any culture.

Capps finds that much similarity exists in the human race. He works hard to show that although the Indian and white cultures are quite different, the people that make up the two cultures bear many similarities. In a letter to Lee, Capps wrote that "all peoples are three-fourths the same and one-fourth a unique culture and racial spirit." He sees a similarity between men and women: "Women are in charge of . . . immediate supplies of food, clothing, shelter, rocking the cradle, intimate family relations" and men "are in charge of the lesser part, hunting, war, ceremony, diplomacy, geopolitics" (Afterword 244).

As Roripaugh suggests, the book compares favorably with other perceptive fictional attempts to "portray the Plains Indian with understanding and artistic skill" (65). He mentions both Jack Schaefer's *The Canyon* and Frederick Manfred's *Conquering Horse*. Some points of comparison with *The Canyon* are enlightening. Like Schaefer, Capps creates an entirely plausible microcosm of Indian life with thinking, flesh-and-blood characters whose actions, thoughts, pains, and triumphs are heartfelt and appropriate for the time and place. Schaefer's Little Bear must face reality on the northern Plains to try to establish a life that will allow him to live as best he can. His acts of bravery such as retrieving the bones of the long-lost warrior so that the spirit can rest, prove the young man's courage and allow him to take a wife. But the emotion he feels is communicated in human terms in much the same way that Capps uses in *A Woman of the People*. Darlene Bellinghausen notes that the parallels with Manfred's *Conquering Horse* are numerous, even though Manfred's work is more mythic, almost supernatural, compared with Capps's truthful rendering of the life of the Indians (2). The most striking accomplishment in all three books is the re-creation of Indian life for modern readers—the folklore, the daily routine, the fears, joys, vices, and religious beliefs of a people. One finds in *A Woman of the People* a short course in Indian culture, with revealing glimpses of intimate details of Indian life on virtually every page.

The White Man's Road

The White Man's Road, which treats life among the Comanches after they have been removed to the reservation, details the plight of Joe Cowbone, a half-breed Comanche Indian in his twenties seeking to accommodate himself to life on the Indian reservation at Fort Sill in Indian Territory (later Oklahoma) around 1890. The novel explores the growing awareness of the protagonist as he tries to find some way of life that he considers productive. Cowbone realizes that he has no distinct direction; he feels he is going in a circle (Ace edition, 150) and searches for the best "road" for himself, feeling it needs to be linear rather than circular.

The various roads Cowbone explores range from the remnants of traditional Indian culture to the radical right of Anglo Christianity. These can be grouped into three fairly distinct categories: older Indians (Great Eagle, Iron Lance, Duncan Bull, and Mad Wolf), young Indians (Freddie Bull and George Longwater, as well as Cowbone's mother), and

Anglo (Reverend Fairchild). But Cowbone follows a fourth example, that of Frank Manybirds, and adapts to his circumstance by incorporating both Indian and Anglo ways into a mode of life that enables him to address successfully the major issues facing him. The reader sees that there is hope for a new generation of Indian represented by Cowbone. His generation must face a transitional phase of Indian life appropriate for the context in which the new generation of Indians must live.

As Cowbone hears the advice of the old Indians, he observes the surroundings and fully realizes that these men and traditional Indian culture have nothing to offer him in his quest for reality. Their recollections are of the time that has little resemblance to the problems that Cowbone faces. The most outrageous example is found in Great Eagle, whose alcoholism and immorality have reduced him to a travesty of Indian life. Lee calls the opening scene of the drunken feast "one of the most disturbing passages ever written about the degradation of reservation life" (*Classics of Texas Fiction* 17).

Iron Lance, another older Indian, nonetheless lacks the bearing and wisdom of an aged warrior. He offers Cowbone various kinds of advice, all archaic and rendered ridiculous because he whittles on his toe nails with a knife while talking to Cowbone. His attitude toward the white man's school is understandable, even his comment that one of the worst influences of school is teaching English to Indians. Cowbone does not feel that what he has learned from Iron Lance is useful to him and leaves disappointed.

The most useless of these advisers is Duncan Bull, an old medicine man who has lost the power of his own medicine and is subject to epileptic fits, but who still either sells or barters his worthless advice to other Indians. Like the other older Indians, Bull seems oblivious of contemporary reality. In contrast, his oldest wife is able to see clearly. She knows that if what Bull says about grease in the medicine tepee is true, he is ruining his own medicine by having the burning candles placed there. This example illustrates the Bull's lack of perception. The epileptic seizure that Bull suffers simply illustrates his lack of control over the ravages of time and his personal deterioration. His day has passed, but, as his old wife says, "He was an important man in his day" (147).

The oldest and understandably most traditional source Cowbone consults is Mad Wolf, whom Cowbone approaches "nervous, wondering, thirstily eager" (183). Mad Wolf, said to be the oldest man who ever lived, is so drawn and shriveled with age that he is dependent on young family members for his basic needs. His pride in never surrendering to the whites has lost its significance because he lives under the security of food and protection furnished by Anglos to the reservation Indians. After the interview with Mad Wolf ends, Cowbone contemplates suicide so that he can go to the "Other Side." Life as he knows it seems empty to Cowbone when compared with that described by Mad Wolf. A voice cries out in Cowbone—"Let me go with you, Mad Wolf" (201). Cowbone also realizes that Mad Wolf's ideas have no bearing on current realities because he does not live in the nomadic days of Comanche life—counting coup, fighting enemies, and stealing horses to prove his manhood and gain honor. Yet he yearns for these earlier days.

Cowbone concludes that these four men have not helped him at all to find a road for his life, but he resolutely keeps seeking. Two other Indian models represented by Freddie Bull and George Longwater are also useless. Cowbone is unable to follow the example of Freddie Bull, who has been to Carlisle Indian School, and he is able to see that Freddie's "road" has cost the young man the respect of his parents. In disgust, Freddie's mother tells Cowbone, "You are worse than Freddie" (147). But Cowbone sees that the ability to read is valuable. For example, he could have understood why Powell's trading post remained closed if he had the skill to read the note on the door, but this avenue is not open to him, even though he learns from Freddie Bull how to read a story and a half from a collection of *Aesop's Fables*. The fables are of no help in guiding him; he has been subjected to other "fables" about life to no avail through the advice that he has sought. By trying, he has acquainted himself with a useful skill that is nonetheless still useless for guiding him in his present dilemma.

Family ties through his Indian mother and white father, who turns out to be the trader Powell, offer little help at the outset. When Cowbone's mother is unable to cope with city life, she seeks another "road" for herself—marriage to a white man. This road is destructive, however, for she and her son are nearly killed, and she loses contact with Powell, her husband who loves her but believes she is dead. When Cowbone takes a job building fence for Powell, he recognizes the ability of the man, especially when Powell mounts a horse bareback from the correct side for an Indian and catches a runaway horse for a cowboy. When Powell refuses to claim Cowbone as his son, Cowbone realizes that this road through his father is denied him.

The route recommended by Frank Manybirds is obviously the road for Cowbone if he wants to succeed in life. Manybird's life proves that the way works. He has been able to adapt to the demands of the world controlled by the white man's law without forfeiting his Indian heritage. He still admires a brave young man who can hunt, and, in line with tradition, he expects horses as gifts when his daughter marries. He instructs his wife on how to clean the turkey Cowbone has killed and to cook it in traditional fashion, not incinerate it like Great Eagle does the sheep. Most important, he tells Cowbone how to adjust to the demands of both worlds. It is not a perfect existence, but his is a sane approach to life as these two find it. When Cowbone helps Lottie chop wood, he performs a chore mainly done by women in traditional culture, but by killing the turkey he performs a warrior's duty.

It is easy to understand that Cowbone cannot abandon traditional Comanche life completely. The horse stealing raid is a futile last gesture similar to that seen in John Graves's "The Last Running." Cowbone's plans for the raid dominate his thinking through much of the book. Part of what Mad Wolf explains to Cowbone is the relationship that the Comanches have always had with horses. Comanches took horses from the gods, he says, and possessing horses is the true test of a Comanche warrior. This, of course, reinforces Cowbone's determination to undertake the horse stealing raid that he has long contemplated. When a chance comes to steal the cavalry horses, Cowbone feels that he is on the right path. The exhilaration of the raid and chase pleases him, but reality, represented by the pursuing soldiers, eventually catches up with him and his friends. When he is wounded in the gunfight with the soldiers but still manages to escape, Cowbone proves his manhood in the Comanche world and can look back on his traditional success. The success of the raid is, however, tinged with irony because the raiders are poorly prepared and armed. They have some supplies hidden before the raid, but the weapons are poor—a bow and arrow, a .22-caliber rifle, and a Sharps .50-caliber buffalo gun, a ponderous weapon, indeed, but one with no ammunition. The raid is a travesty of the lightning raids of Comanche warriors in the days of fearless depredation, and the fact that they are followed by Rev. Fairchild renders the whole scene almost comic. Lottie's offer to bandage Cowbone's wound leads to the resumption of their love making and then to their marriage, so the raid is certainly not a complete failure. But Cowbone is certain that this road is not one that provides a rewarding life. He loses his booty, and the effects of the wound continue to bother him when he tries to ride the bucking horses, thus assuring that he cannot work too long as a bronc buster.

The other "road" is that of the white man, which the Indians closely identify with religious faith and practice. For example, they call the preacher the Comanche equivalent of "road teller" and the church "road house." The latter usage always brings unexplained laughter from whites. This misunderstanding causes the Indians to withdraw from the white man's religion and shows the Anglo's insensitivity toward the Indian.

The white man's road demonstrated by the Rev. Fairchild is too extreme for Cowbone. Fairchild wants to convert Cowbone to Christianity and encourages him to report to the soldiers his part in the theft of the horses. Long-suffering and sincere, Fairchild does not want to understand the old ways but wants instead to impose the new ways on Cowbone or, better yet, have Cowbone impose them on himself to replace traditional culture. Cowbone finally follows Fairchild's advice to turn himself in to the soldiers and is locked up in the jail at the fort. He recognizes that he cannot follow his own choice in life with the chance that his role in the crime might cause him problems later in life. It is ironic that he has only a pocket knife when he turns himself in, for the knife was an important implement—and symbol—to an Indian. He does not have the long, sharp warrior's knife; his has only a folding blade, not one open for action at all times but most often stored, unready for use. Similarly, Cowbone owns a Winchester rifle but has no ammunition, a mute symbol of his impotence. The angry officer's lecture to Cowbone on the nature of stealing, as white men understand it, is ludicrous because the military officer shows no cognizance of the traditional way that Comanches have proved their manhood—by stealing horses. The whole situation of his confession, imprisonment, and release is ridiculous to Cowbone, and to the reader.

When Cowbone earns his horses in order to offer a traditional dowry for Lottie, he has modified traditional Comanche culture. When he has Rev. Fairchild perform a Christian wedding ceremony and takes up farming on his own land on the reservation to establish a home for his family, he is assuming at least a semblance of Anglo life as part of his existence. He accepts his father into his home and lets him help Cowbone and Lottie's son learn to read and write. Cowbone helps teach his son to read in order to learn the skill himself. He sees that education is a necessity for a young man, thus contradicting the advice of Duncan Bull and Iron Lance.

Cowbone has found a method of living in this world by adapting his culture to the present. He rejects the traditional life that would keep him at odds with himself and with contemporary life. He is determined not to be like a bee after the honey tree has been cut down. Instead, Cowbone becomes a modern Indian. He will not face the demands of counting coup and stealing horses, but he will deal with his Comanche bravery, pride in himself, his family, his band, and the Comanche people. Cowbone has a chance because he finds a way to follow his personal version of the white man's road by doing what successful people on the frontier across America did: he adapts what is necessary but does not abandon traditional values and beliefs. Cowbone's path is no longer circular.

This novel is not a chronicle of various massacres and cavalry charges as one might expect a novel to be when Comanches and soldiers are involved. Instead, it is a character study of the plight of a young man—of whatever culture—seeking to determine what to do with his life. The rich mixture of traditional and modern elements that Capps has worked into the narrative certainly adds to the effectiveness of the story and of its historical content. One of the sad comments is the paucity of choices offered to this young man, a situation quite real for the Indian of this period, for these people were indeed lost between two worlds—the traditional one and the new one that they had to face.

Capps closes the novel with the following passage detailing the "road" taken by most of the Indians:

> Whatever strengths in their blood had made them once lords of a great land were in them still. No people in all of the history of mankind has faced a more difficult and painful dilemma. They wavered in anguish and a void between two worlds. Their frustrations and sadness and

> hope were beyond the comprehension of those who had not faced it. Then one by one they packed their dearest treasures from out of the past, made bundles of them, took these bundles upon their backs and set out for the journey on what they called the white man's road. (319)

Capps has been true to this time and place. Lee's contention that place is important to the work is true, and, as he suggests, this use of setting is found in "the best regional fiction—that which rises above localism toward the universal" (Afterword 314).

As Lee notes, "Capps wants the reader to see that the white man's road is no life for a Comanche, no life for a person who has known the spirit of the plains and has ridden after the buffalo" (Afterword 315). The author's attitude is one of sympathetic support for a people faced with a monumental adjustment to make, and Capps depicts a rational man exploring various options before making his existential leap to the desired path.

These three Indian novels contain many of Capps's ideas and values about the Indian of the West. The history, folklore, and cultural value of Indians are woven into these readable, well-written, and historically accurate pieces of fiction. That Capps knew his Indian history well is demonstrated in three historical studies discussed in the next chapter.

4

THE HISTORICAL NONFICTION

Capps produced an extensive body of nonfiction that includes the three book-length works on Indians in the West discussed in this chapter, as well as parts of three travel guides, numerous articles and reviews, and an edited volume. This work is representative of Capps's canon in content, style, and areas of interest, and it presents another side of the talent of Capps the writer. In this material, Capps retains his professional integrity and reveals the wide range of interest and adaptability of one dedicated to his craft and to his materials.

The extensive research that Capps conducted on Indians manifested itself in two anecdotal histories of Plains Indians—*The Indians* (1973) and *The Great Chiefs* (1974) in the Time-Life Series on the American West—and the remarkable *The Warren Wagontrain Raid* (1974), unusual in that it is heavily fictionalized. In these, Capps's view is at least objective if not tacitly supportive of the cause and problem of the red men. He certainly does not belittle them.

The Time-Life Books

Although both *The Indians* and *The Great Chiefs* were works for hire and are presented in formats characteristic of the Time-Life series designed for the general public, they also are typical of the more serious work that Capps has done. The first of these books, *The Indians,* offered Capps the opportunity to tell numerous stories of the native Americans and also to include historical sketches that give a collage designed to communicate a general image of the subject. The book has seven chapters—"The Faces of a Proud People," "The Wide World of the Horse Indians," "An Ingenious Way To Live," "Seeking Help from the Spirits," "The White Man's Invasion," "Conquering the Peace," and "Confrontation on the Plains"—and surveys the general history of the Indians from before the whites came until the Indians' greatest moment in their latter days in confrontation against the whites. Capps weaves into the historical vignettes much specific detail about Indian life. He describes clothing, jewelry, and horse accoutrements; he explains a great deal about the training and breeding of horses, hunting buffalo, making arrows, cooking and drying meat, and naming children; he presents splendid expositions of games and toys and courtship practices; and he tells the nonspecialist about dressing hides and making tepees, funeral rites, religious rituals, and even the effect of Manifest Destiny and broken treaties on the Indians. The closing segment of the book, which covers the Battle of the Little Bighorn, is characteristically done by Capps with great thoroughness, spirit, and excitement, and with careful attention to historical accuracy.

A companion volume, *The Great Chiefs,* focuses on several of the most notable leaders of the western Indian tribes, such as the Kiowas White Bear and Sitting Bear, the Apaches Cochise and Geronimo, the Comanche Quanah Parker, the Eastern Shoshoni Washakie, the Nez Perce Chief Joseph, and the Sioux Sitting Bull. He includes sketches of other Indians such as Captain Jack of the Modocs, who in an outbreak in 1872 killed General Edward Canby—the only man of his rank killed in the Indian wars—with a bullet to the head during a peace conference. Capps closes his second volume with the low point of the Indians' life, the Battle of Wounded Knee, in which Sioux Indians under Chief Bigfoot, several of whom were followers of the recently deceased Sitting Bull, were shot down by soldiers on the plains of Wyoming and were left to be covered by a snowstorm.

The photographs and illustrations in the books are illuminating and striking, and the artwork is characteristic—some of it presented in double-page panorama. Pictures of weapons, tools, and games strengthen the presentation and offer a reasonably complete view of what Indian life in the Old West was like.

Even if these works of more than 230 pages each were done for hire, the research material that Capps incorporated into his novels served a useful purpose for him, and the research on these books no doubt contributed to the contents of later ones. Several of the incidents in his other works appear in these books. Events in the life of Satank (also known as Sitting Bear), one of the principal figures in *The Warren Wagontrain Raid,* are treated in considerable detail as Capps describes his leadership skills, his part in the killing of the forty-eight Cheyenne members of the Bow String Society whose scalped bodies were left in a row on the prairie, his gift of 250 horses to the Cheyennes during a later peace conference, his wearing the black belt of the Society of the Ten Bravest, and his dramatic self-imposed death at the hands of soldiers at Fort Sill where he literally gnawed the flesh from his hands in order to free them from the shackles and then pointed the jammed rifle at the soldiers before he was cut down in a hail of bullets.

Much of the material used in *Women Chief* grew out of the research for these two books, especially *The Indians,* which appeared six years before the novel was printed. In the novel, Capps cites the work of Denig on the Crow Indians. This government document contains the principal narrative account of Woman Chief, and many of the details that appear in the novel also appear in the historical account. For example, Woman Chief's insistence that she go on the buffalo hunt is thwarted only when the leader of the hunt threatens to kill her horse and whip her with a quirt. This punishment is given in *The Indians* as that to be expected of a man who hunts during the "no hunt time" for the Crows. In addition, the Indians' practice of gathering turnips included in the novel is explained in this volume.

The style of writing is distinctively that of Capps. No lapse of talent is noticeable here. Also, one finds use of the same techniques that enlivened *The Warren Wagontrain Raid,* for he interpolates remarks and reactions of the historical figures—a feature of *The Warren Wagontrain Raid* for which he has been criticized.

One example of Capps's interpolations can be seen in the section on Crazy Horse, leader of the Sioux during the Fetterman Massacre. In describing a battle in which the Indians lured the soldiers out of protective cannon range and slaughtered seventy-eight soldiers and two civilians on December 21, 1866, near Fort Phil Kearny, Capps writes, "Crazy Horse must have been praying; 'Come on! Come on!'" (*The Great Chiefs* 196). Fetterman had earlier bragged that with eighty men he could "ride through the whole Sioux nation." Crazy Horse proved Fetterman incapable of riding more than a few miles from the post.

Similarly, at the big peace conference of 1840, Capps puts words into the mouth of Indian children, who might have climbed into the trees to see the approaching Indians:

> They called back and forth to those on the ground. One can imagine their shrill cries. "I see them coming! Yes! Straight out there! A village of people! Pack horses! People riding! Loads on travois poles!" "How many loose horses?" "It looks like a hundred—more than a hundred!" And from another tree: "Look to the left! Under the dust! Many horses!" "Loose horses? Count them!" "It must be five hundred!" And from still another tree watcher—"Eeee! A thousand coming over the ridge! They keep coming! More than a thousand! And I see dust a way back!" (*The Great Chiefs* 18)

By imagining such dialogue, Capps enriches the story for the audience, the contribution of a talented novelist so immersed in his materials that he feels the characters need to speak out more than a century later in order to live again and set the record straight. Capps goes beyond just recounting history in other ways: he interprets events and plans, offering insights and citing parallels and implications. For example, in *The Indians* he comments on the plan of a group of idealists who theorized a solution to the Indian problem in the West—put all of them on four to seven reservations, give each one eighty acres of "good land," and make every effort to civilize them. Of this plan, Capps offers the following perceptive criticism:

> But the well-meant plan only showed once again that many of the reformers and idealists were almost as limited in their views as the white war hawks whom they despised. To put the numerous distinct tribes of the West on so few reservations would inevitably have caused frustration and confusion; much Western land was so arid that eighty acres would not support a person equipped with only the farming implements and methods of the time; and, most important of all, many Indians simply did not want to be civilized or to accept the whites' definition of civilization. (*The Indians* 200)

He offers the following comment on the effect of such thinking:

> The ultimate effect of the Eastern humanitarians on the frontier crisis was difficult to assess

> with any accuracy. Undoubtedly they did some good. Without their idealistic pressure, the proposal for exterminating the last free fighting Indians might have been put into action. Yet it was clear that the humanitarians did not understand all of the realities of the Plains Indians' way of life. The Sioux were a proud, conquering people. What warrior would follow a plow or do woman's work because some white man said he should? (*The Indians* 200)

Capps's inclusion of the rich folkloric details of social customs and other elements of Indian life that he covers in these two nonfiction works served him well in enriching his writing and his understanding of the socioeconomic and personal side of the Indians. His infatuation with the Indians of the American West forms an important part of his literary and historical output. His grasp of materials is obvious and his interpolation of them true to life and accurate.

The Warren Wagontrain Raid

Capps's research led to a highly significant but controversial historical work, *The Warren Wagontrain Raid,* a serious attempt to give the most complete and accurate accounting to date of events sparked by a raid that a war party of Kiowa Indians launched on a wagontrain near Jacksboro in North Texas on May 18, 1871. In 304 pages of text, notes, maps, photographs, and index, Capps explores the subject by dividing it into chapters clearly focused on the various elements affected by the raid. He first develops the three principal parts—the Indians who raided, the soldiers who pursued the Indians, and the freighters who were attacked. The next chapter deals with a description of the attack itself, and the following chapter with the pursuit by soldiers intent on punishing the Indians. He then devotes a chapter to Indian agent Lawrie Tatum in order to lead into the next chapter, which concerns the confrontation between the soldiers and the Indians at Fort Sill. Chapter Eight, "The Dungeon," depicts the three Indian leaders incarcerated in a basement at Fort Sill. The next chapters deal with the settlers, the trial, the imprisonment, and then a major council discussion followed by a time of freedom for the Indians, and finally the alliance that saw the Indian and Anglo problem progress to another set of concerns as a new level of civilization came to North Texas and Oklahoma.

Capps's interpretation of the personalities, especially of the Indians, provides some penetrating insights. For example, through the mind of Lawrie Tatum, Capps recalls a time in 1869 or 1870 that points to the poignant irony of the behavior of the whites and the Indians. At that time, Satank led a band of followers to attack a herd of cattle near the North Canadian River in the Cheyenne-Arapaho reservation. The Indians charged into the cattle, shot arrows into the herd, and generally created havoc in the ensuing stampede. Two hundred of the cattle destined to become food at the Indian reservation were wantonly and senselessly slaughtered. Chief Satanta later recalled the incident and noted that this was done to reflect similar outrageous actions of the whites in regard to the Indians' "cattle," the buffalo, which were slaughtered for sport and later only for their hides. The lack of perception on the part of the whites is typical, much as is the difference in meaning between a "massacre" and a "victory." The definition depends on which side one fights for or favors. The poignant irony of the killing of the cattle, when juxtaposed later in Satank's memory, makes the point clearly.

The pro-Indian side of the book shows the gullibility of 2d Lt. Robert Goldthwaite Carter, aged twenty-six, post adjutant, and an "eager-beaver" who was conned by his brother officers into trying to find a cannon to fire a salute when General Sherman arrived at Fort Richardson the day of the attack. A "serious-minded major" stopped the ruse and sent Carter on his real mission—"to take fifteen men along the road west, meet the General-in-Chief of the Army, welcome him, and escort him back to the post" (First edition, 43). There is some comic relief in the otherwise very serious book. Capps makes Carter, who later wrote an inaccurate version of the events, the butt of the humor.

Capps is not reluctant to broaden the perspective of the book to include details of other atrocities committed in the same area. Perhaps the most poignant is that of the Negro Britt Johnson, whose wife and children were kidnapped by Kiowas. Johnson managed to steal his family back but was later killed in the Elm Creek Raid near the spot where the wagontrain would be attacked three months later. The Kiowas knew Johnson, for, as Capps notes: "Britt's body was surrounded by a hundred and nine spent cartridges; Indian hair was clenched in his dead hand. Reports said that the Kiowas must have recognized him, for his body was more mutilated than those of his three companions" (141).

A second incident developed at some length is the kidnapping of young Millie Durgan, captured at age eighteen months in the Elm Creek Raid, where Britt's family was taken. Not until 1930, sixty-five years later, did Millie Durgan come back to Young County. She had grown up a Kiowa; had seen Kit Carson attack a Kiowa camp; had for a foster father a member of the Society of the Ten Bravest; and had become known to her adopted people as Saint-to-Hoodle Goombi. Her offspring included five children, thirty-two grandchildren, and twelve great grandchildren. As an old woman she toured Texas schools telling her story to the youngsters. She also became a member of an association of early-day Indian fighters.

Capps's interest in history is more apparent in this book than in his works of pure fiction. He grew up not far from the site of the raid and visited the location on several occasions. His use of specific dates, locations, and manners of people involved creates an aura of authenticity that was no doubt real to him because of his familiarity with the site. Not until one checks Capps's notes does it become apparent how much research went into the book, how much he incorporated, and how much he interpolated in some cases. The notes—nearly forty pages of them—are in narrative style without distracting numbers in the text. He not only gives his sources but elaborates on their validity or lack of it and compares various accounts of different incidents. He relied on details from James Auchiah, Satanta's grandson, who provided information on the man as well as the chief's arrow lance. Barbara Ledbetter, a well-informed historian of the area, especially of Fort Belknap where she is an archivist, also served as a resource. Capps cites details of army activities from microfilm copies of contemporary reports from the area in which the action occurred. In his discussion of sources, Capps writes, "My notes are not comprehensive. They are intended to deal with controversial points, as a defense of my inferences and deductions, and as justification for information not covered in previous accounts. In the case of published material, editions most easily available to me have been used" (257). This is no haphazardly written account, but is instead a delicately handled narrative written by a master of his material.

What Capps accomplishes in *The Warren Wagontrain Raid* is a remarkable feat—a re-creation, as nearly as the facts and an informed imagination can produce it, of the actions, principal individuals, milieu, and consequences of this act of daring. Capps's extensive research into the primary and secondary sources—he recounts the thrill of seeing a reproduction of a letter in Sherman's own handwriting—gives him as solid a basis as one can develop, after the fact, to write this account. The book is a coherent, readable, thoroughly enjoyable, and informative rendering of the affair and is an outstanding combination of fact and fiction.

This fictionalizing of history, however, has concerned many readers who feel far more comfortable when fiction and history remain clearly distinct. Three notable authorities have criticized Capps's fictionalizing in this work. One of these is C.L.

Sonnichsen, one of Capps's friends and strong supporters in reviews of his other books and an astute commentator on both the fiction and history of the American West. Indeed, he spent a distinguished career deeply involved in both, as his work *The Ambidextrous Historian* suggests. In his review in *Western American Literature,* Sonnichesen raises the question of whether Capps's methodology is sound and asks if Capps would "have done better to write straight fiction with a factual background, as he did in *A Woman of the People,* or plain pedestrian history" (60). He goes on to ask if Capps has "any right to turn his imagination loose when he is trying to get at historical fact" (61). Of the documentation, Sonnichsen notes: "The serious student will also be disturbed by Capps's footnotes, which he uses to chat about his problems [and] argue about credibility" (61).

Similarly, in *Southwestern Historical Quarterly,* Wayne Gard, himself no stranger to both fiction and history, after applauding Capps for the quality of research in the book, faults Capps for being "unable to restrain the novelist's habit of adding imagined details and dialogue and telling what he assumes were the motives and thoughts of his characters." Gard's final judgment of the book is that it would have been "better history if the author had limited his writing to ascertainable facts" (103).

In his review in *Western Historical Quarterly,* William H. Leckie finds "objectionable" the author's efforts to record the thoughts of Satanta, Satank, and Big Tree: "One is on thin ice at any moment one presumes to read the thoughts of another and particularly when the latter is of a different culture and several generations removed in time" (188).

Capps is not insensitive to this point of concern, but the approach he used was not one taken lightly. In his "Preface" to the original edition of the book, he admits that he has "not hesitated to proceed further in interpretation than would the professional historian" (xiv). He goes on to say that he doubts any reader will be apt to misinterpret what is "documentable fact, what is inferred fact, and what is imagined detail such as reconstructed dialogue" (xiv). Obviously, that statement did not satisfy the critics, nor has the issue died. In an "Apologia" included in the 1989 Southern Methodist University Press reprint of *The Warren Wagontrain Raid,* Capps responds to the problem of fictionalizing: He asks, "Am I . . . substituting my imagination for historical fact, or am I following fact carefully and merely adding fiction elements which seem true?" Then he poses these notions: "To whom does history belong? To historians, in the kind of closed circle, or is it a good idea at some point to get out of the ivory tower and produce writings to interest a larger public? Does the general reader deserve and appreciate the documented facts along with interpretation, even thoughtful fictionalizing?" He presses the question, "Do those who produce strictly 'factual' history always get the facts right?" (xiv). The answer seems obvious. He furthers his notion when he says, "Should I have presented [the material] as a novel, with no documentation? Then a number of historians, amateurs or professionals, would have said: 'Good writing, but he has the sequence of events wrong'" (xvi). He cites as an example a key error in Marcy's journal, which, through ambiguous wording, led many to believe that the attack occurred on the morning of May 17 rather than May 18. Capps notes other errors propagated by additional writers on the subject and feels he has defended his actions and corrected several errors in fact.

Near the end of his defense, Capps writes at some length about his approach: "The attraction of the subject to me lay in the variety of points of view: the settlers, the Indians, the Indian service, the army. A reader, in order to get the complete truth about the total situation, would need to read several books about the Kiowas and think about them. But that some people are not considering any Indian point of view is clear from the sources. . . . The reader who had not studied native American people in their situation would never see the whole truth of The Warren Wagontrain Raid." The concluding paragraph of this piece shows that Capps has not changed his mind: "In any case, I should admit that I have profited much over the years from the work of good historians. Their accounts and documentation are invaluable as a starting point for every kind of writing" (xviii). In a letter to this author concerning the "Apologia," Capps writes, "I honestly do not feel highly partisan about the fictionalizing issue and don't blame anyone for disagreeing with me" (9 December 1988).

If Capps erred in his methods, and not everyone thinks that he did, he did so in the direction of his chosen craft—fiction. But he stayed with the facts because of his belief that "the real people who lived in the American West in the Nineteenth Century have been victim of too much fiction passing for fact" (Apologia xvi). Elmer Kelton, a writer of quality fiction about the West and a well-informed historian, has frequently said that fiction allows him the opportunity to bring events and people in history to life. Capps has pushed the limits for historians, but surely the serious student of the historical facts of this small but admittedly significant development in the history of the American frontier will read all the available versions and accounts and make a decision on the validity of the information in each. In this case, Capps's book is invaluable because of the historical data included as well as the contribution of bringing to life the principal figures involved, white and red. Even Sonnichsen's largely negative review includes the comment that part of Capps's "success is undoubtedly due to his willingness to explore the minds of his native characters, inventing conversations, and analyzing motives as he goes along. There can be no doubt that he is a master of vivid narrative and an expert developer of character as a successful and skillful novelist has to be" (61).

The materials that Capps spent long months researching have cultural as well as historical significance. In his "Apologia," he writes of the event and the milieu in which it happened: "Here we have native people with a hunter-gatherer economy; such people have for many thousands of years clashed with and often defeated those with a village-farmer economy. Then at some point the farmers started winning part of the time—more recently all of the time. The situation may be the basis for the Cain-and-Abel myth" (xiii). Capps sees archetypal potential in the material that serves as the basis for this book.

In addition to this archetypal significance, the event had historical impact because it may well have been a turning point in the history of the Indian situation in the West. Since General Sherman was Commander of the U.S. Army for the twelve years during which the Indian policy in the West moved to one of extermination rather than pacification, it may be that his close call as the object of the raid, his first-hand experience with the horror of the raid, and his acquaintance with the principals involved may have shaped his view that extinction was the most desirable solution to the Indian problem in western America.

What Capps does in the book is to present all sides of the story for readers who do not have the time or perhaps the interest to read enough material to understand the milieu in which the events occurred. It seems likely that the perceptive reader will be able to distinguish among "documentable facts," "inferred fact," and "imagined detail," and enjoy the account.

Capps's nonfiction forms a major segment of his literary output and fits in with his place as a professional writer, a high-sounding title but one that required him to support a family on the income he could derive from the efforts of his pen. The central impression generated by this part of his canon is that even in these histories, Capps was as dedicated to quality writing, accurate research, flowing prose, and the other requirements of fine writing as he was in his novels.

5

THE WRITER ON HIS CRAFT

Although critics often apply the pejorative label "regionalist" to anyone choosing to write about the West, most serious commentators on western writing see Capps as a serious writer who has consciously elected to interpret the universal human experience in the Trans-Mississippi West, particularly the South Plains. He has shown a strong commitment to interpretive fiction and history, and to the artistic quality necessary to maintain the demanding level of performance acceptable to him. Capps has striven to assure that artistic quality is a guiding force in his work.

Capps says that the serious Western, old or new, tries to say something about the universal human condition and, if successful, is not strictly entertainment. "I try to slip a little message in between the lines," Capps has said in an interview. "I don't try to hit the reader over the head with it, but I've got something I want to say in the context of that story." Even though he has set these stories in the West, he believes that he is "just as serious as any other writer ever was." Capps is convinced that the field he has used for his work is a fertile one for serious writing: "I believe there is room for such work in this great country west of the Mississippi, for so much has happened here that you can find material on which to use the techniques of fiction. There are enough details of action and character and such as to write something that displays universals about the human predicament on this planet, as much as the Greeks or Shakespeare or anybody else did" (Interview). He continues by noting that more than craft will be apparent in this kind of writing; if the work is successful, the inspiration and craftsmanship will produce artistic novels that should be memorable experiences for the well-read person, regardless of the setting or outcome of the story.

Since Capps is dedicated to the serious Western, his criticism of the formula Western is severe. He has described such fiction as hastily done, superficial writing about the West. An illustrative example of this notion comes from an incident when his youngest son, then about eight years old, came in from school and began watching a rerun of one of the adventures of the Lone Ranger on television. After about two minutes the son stood up and said, "Dad gum, same old thing time after time; I'm going outside and play." Capps notes that the kind of repetitive escapism associated with television characterizes formula fiction, which is a kind of stereotyped daydream. He says, "How can a writer daydream somebody else's daydreams again and again?"

Most formula Westerns focus on gun-toting horsemen, cowboys, frontier sheriffs, outlaws, blazing six-guns, running horses, range wars, Indian fights, and stagecoach and bank robberies. Serious fiction can conceivably deal with such action-oriented stories, but when this material figures prominently in the work, action often dominates the other qualities and leads to omissions in content. Formula Westerns often omit the mundane, everyday details of life in favor of over-dramatized escapades. Most settled rural dwellers on the frontier, for example, worked hard to have a garden for fresh vegetables, a flock of chickens, and a small field of a forage crop for winter livestock feed in order to survive. These people lived close to the soil. Inclusion of this kind of detail is significant to quality fiction. In fact, in his review of Bryan Woolley's novel *Sam Bass,* Capps praises the author because "the appeal of the novel comes from a sense of reality of a time and a place and a way of life. We smell the wood smoke and the coffee boiling on an open fire. We come to accept sleeping on the ground as natural. We know that groceries were available and would keep and could be carried on a pack horse. We understand that a really good horse, decked out in a fine saddle and bridle, was to a young man like a classy, sporty automobile today" (4K).

In formula Westerns the plots are simple, fast-paced, and rarely complicated by well-developed subplots. The conflict is worked out in a range of fifty to sixty thousand words. The focus is on action, or the possibility of action, not on character development. The confrontations are between clearly good or evil characters who blatantly represent one extreme or the other, not the human middle ground of real life. To many people, the powder burner is the only valid type of Western; works that vary from the pattern are interlopers—charlatans masquerading as the genuine article.

Capps feels that many areas of experience in the West should be made the subject of western fiction. Of the vast materials available to the western writer, such as the experiences of the fur hunters, the miners, the Indian wars, the cattleman, frontier commerce, the homesteader, the transition of the frontier to the town, and the days of the railroad development, Capps would add the relationship between Indians, the Indians on the reservation, and the relationship of the Indians with the Anglos. These materials offer sufficient complication to make interesting fiction. This Capps sees as more productive than rehearsing the trite myth of the cowboy, usually misrepresented and glamorized far beyond what it actually was. Of this and other such exaggerations, Capps wryly states: "Things aren't what they used to be, and they never were." ("The Western," The Governor's Sesquicentennial Literary Conference.)

Since Capps does not write traditional Westerns, readers do not find in his novels the popular heroes often found in fiction and film such as the Lone Ranger. These heroes are, as Elmer Kelton often has described such figures, seven feet tall and invincible. Kelton's description fits the heroes of Louis L'Amour, but not his own or those of Capps. Like Kelton, Capps is interested in well-developed characterizations, plausible figures who remind readers of their own existence. In an extensive evaluation of Andy Adams's classic cowboy story, *The Log of a Cowboy,* Capps praises Adams for accurately depicting the old-time cowboy as "a fun-loving, sentimental, easy-going, hard-working, skilled laborer." He says further, "A reader who is weary of cheap stereotypes and the heroic cowboy myth finds Adams's people delightful" ("A Critical Look" 2). But he is not reluctant to criticize Adams as well. He feels that Adams fails to reveal the deeper truth that people are individuals—that each one is different. And he says that showing this difference lies at the heart of all good fiction and that this characteristic is far more important than authenticity, which is not the crucial criterion of good fiction. He cites as an example Shakespeare, who was an "atrocious historian" but whose skills at character development were superb.

Capps admires complexity as well as diversity in character. When planning *The Trail to Ogallala,* he admits he was influenced by Jack London's short story "To Build a Fire," in which man is viewed as a "puny" force and a dog as the strong figure. But Capps believes that the exact opposite is also true—"namely that human determination and competence often master Nature or often use her for human purposes rather than succumbing to her. This attitude about the right and the ability of man to dominate non-human Nature is strong in Judeo-Christian thought and perhaps the major assumption in traditional Western writing" ("Breaking into Print" 1).

Capps followed his own rules of artistic quality in his work. For example, one of his strongest characters is the title figure in *Sam Chance.* Chance is far too human to be a hero in the usual sense of the word. Instead, he, among other "human" responses, contributes to the death of his wife with a kind of mental cruelty, a selfishness with which she cannot cope. In his discussion of Chance at the 1986 Governor's Sesquicentennial Literary Conference in Denton, Texas, Capps said, "Sam Chance did a lot of bad things. I created him as an interesting character, not as a hero. I believe that any character is more interesting if he has some weakness or evil; this makes him seem like a real person." Capps believes that fictional characters should be able to make mistakes and suffer for those mistakes, and the reader can then identify with the character as being real. Among memorable "real" characters in Capps's novels are Charley Blankenship in *The True Memoirs of Charley Blankenship,* Helen Morrison in *A Woman of the People,* Joe Cowbone in *The White Man's Road,* and the title character in *Woman Chief.*

Capps's critical tastes were evident long before he published his first novel. In 1951, in a review of James Jones's *From Here to Eternity,* Capps wrote: "If a writer wishes to give a truthful account of army life, he must deal with many things which are not mentioned by ladies and gentlemen in polite conversation. But it seems that an author who demands the right to be realistic should also accept the responsibility of being consistently realistic. *From Here to Eternity* has highly romantic aspects" (n.p.). In a review in *Western American Literature* of *Pioneer Surveyor–Frontier Lawyer: The Personal Narrative of O.W. Williams: 1877–1902* (ed. S.D. Myres), Capps praises Williams for writing what he knew was important even though he likely knew it would not sell well. He also compliments Williams's "dependable impression of a broad and perceptive mind" (312). The artist must pay a price for the right to be truthful.

Like Elmer Kelton, Capps has a deep and abiding love for history as a basis for quality fiction. To many readers, history and fiction may seem poles apart, but at heart they are not that much different. Edmund Morgan, a noted American historian, defines the writing of history as "the creative ordering of past events" (v). Obviously, historians must write in such a way as to communicate ideas and describe events based on verifiable facts. In short, they tell the verifiable story of a particular set of events in a specific time.

Fiction, on the other hand, is a narrative composed of characters, events, and, to some degree, places created by an artist to reflect life in a particular time and hold it up for inspection. Although the story may be based on ascertainable facts, the material is nonetheless fictionalized. Historical fiction provides a distinct link between history as Morgan has defined it and fiction as Capps has created it. Capps's dual roles as historian and novelist are linked in him because of the influence of accurate historical materials on the plots, setting, and characters in his novels. According to Lee, Capps "is a historical novelist in the best sense of that vague literary term; that is, he is not a writer of costume novels but an author who meticulously recreates time past" ("Benjamin Capps" in *Fifty Western Writers* 45). Lee goes on to say that Capps's "depiction of the culture of the whites and the Indians makes [him] one of America's best historical novelists" (45). Similarly, Capps's unusual historical piece, *The Warren Wagontrain Raid,* has been criticized by Leckie for reading too much like a novel (188), but Capps has balanced his approach to written narrative by presenting even in his historical material a story that breathes and moves with life. In each of his narratives, Capps offers believable characters, accurately depicted settings, and a well-developed plot with a beginning, a middle, and an end. His aim in creating a fictional world for his story is to present the culture of a people because, according to Lee, the culture is the "totality of their lives: their traditions, their beliefs, their folklore, their views of the world, their attempts to adapt to their environment" ("Benjamin Capps" in *Fifty Western Writers* 45).

That Capps is well aware of this broad concern is apparent in his review of Kelton's *The Good Old Boys,* in which Capps praises Kelton's depiction of the setting by saying that "if a reader grew up in the ranching country of the South Plains he will be filled with nostalgia by this book. If he didn't grow up there, he will be filled with the conviction that this must have been the way it really was" (9F). Capps's praise reveals his admiration for art based on actuality, whether in his own work or in that of someone else. Capps does the research so well that if someone checks the details, Capps will not be found lacking. He says that a reader has a right to find the correct governor's name used in a novel set at a particular time and in a specific place, and he expects this kind of veracity from what he reads. For example, after pointing out errors in fact in Paul Foreman's *Quanah,* a fictional study of the famous half-white Comanche chief, Capps says, "This book is not recommended for accuracy in history, geography, ethnology, psychology, or even as a model for the craft of fiction" (n.p.). Although Foreman complained to the editors of the *Dallas Morning News* about Capps's attack on the novel, Capps held firm to his criticism because Capps knew the historical facts of Quanah Parker's life and saw the discrepancies in Foreman's account. Capps, like other historical novelists, may compress or expand a given incident and improvise on a character in history or even create a composite character based on several people he has known or read about. But the piece, be it fiction or history, will ring with authenticity. Capps adds that "the deeper truth is that no extensive literature will be based on the mere realistic description of the work of a skilled laborer. When you've punched one cow you've punched them all. But the West was a thousand times as big as the cowboy" ("The Promise of Western Fiction, Part 3" 24).

Capps has read widely and believes that reading is the most productive way to learn about life. In an interview, Capps once said, "Reading should shape your vision of life whether you are a writer or a reader. What . . . is writing for? I agree that it is an art. The writer combines technique with some kind of ideals of truth. He hopes that through the piece of writing the people may live more abundantly. In other words, it serves to raise the reader's horizon." Capps continues by asking what a person should really strive to do. "Live a really narrow life, even if you live to be a hundred years old, or a rich life? You see more things when you read. Everything means more to you. You can better understand people's positions and predicaments. Although we may not believe everything we find in what we read, we compare it to who we are, what we know, and what we do next week, even though we don't [make the comparison] formally. Somewhere in the back of our minds we make those assessments."

Capps began developing his views early in life through reading and personal observation. In elementary school, he hid on top of the cow shed and, as he wrote in an unpublished typescript to this author, "sailed the seven seas with Melville and Conrad, prowled the jungle with Tarzan, dared the cold north with London, laughed with Mark Twain." As a voracious young reader, he worked through everything available: the Bible, the works of Theodore Roosevelt, Zane Grey, Horatio Alger, Jr., and whatever else he could find (Commire 30). He read all of Shakespeare's plays before he entered high school. One of the reasons for this, he says, is that "We didn't have much to do. I can remember ten years without even a radio" (Barnett 23). He was particularly influenced by Mark Twain, although he acknowledges admiring the work of John Steinbeck and William Faulkner. In a list of the ten great short stories of the world, he included stories written by Chekov, Gogol, Chaucer, Dickens, Melville, Hawthorne, and Welty. Capps did not stop reading at the end of high school and has continued to read widely. As a member of a group of readers for the Western Writers of America's journal *The Roundup,* he read and reviewed many new books each year. He also reviewed books for the *Fort Worth Star-Telegram* and other outlets and he says, "There would be some months that I would get a dozen books and review three or four of them" (Interview). He had a good working relationship with Leonard Sanders, book review editor for the *Star-Telegram,* and for a time, Capps wrote reviews virtually every week for that paper. Now, however, he says he no longer reads Westerns; instead, he prefers medieval and ancient history.

As to why he began writing novels about the West, Capps recalled in an interview, "My English teacher when I was fourteen said that a person should write about what that person knows." Here his observations about life became an advantage. He says, "I know the solitary spaces and things like that. I have an advantage over writers in New York or Philadelphia or Atlanta because I am writing about my own roots. Until I was sixteen years old we heated and cooked with wood [so] I can relate to people who go out in a wagon, pulled by mules, and haul wood and chop it up and put it in a wood fire and cook dinner." Because he lived it, this sense of reality is apparent in his books.

Capps told the audience at the session on the Western at the Governor's Sesquicentennial Literary Conference that the material he has used is some of "the greatest material that anybody can have," and he hopes to "respect it and have the talent to use it." Of this material, readily available to the writer of the Western, Capps says, "Settlement in what is now the United States started in the Southwest under the influence of northern New Spain. It has gone all across this continent, and it has not been very long since it started. All this mixing and mingling of people with different cultures did not start all that long ago. We are not talking about the ancient Mesopotamia; we are talking about our own land." He asks, rhetorically, "How long ago was it when people were spearing buffalo here in Texas with stone-tipped spears? . . . probably not more than a hundred and fifty years. That is not very long in human history, and yet we have that as part of the possibilities for our fiction."

Access to this material is easy. For example, Capps cites as unusually perceptive a book by Elizabeth Johns called *Storms Brewed in Other Men's Worlds*. The narrative begins with Coronado and goes up to about 1800. In it one finds detailed "the activities of two hundred and fifty years of people mixing and mingling in the Southwest. Twenty different Indian peoples plus the French and the Spanish and to some extent the English with their own separate religions and attitudes and economies had their influence. Some of them were enemies, and some of them were friends. Some of them made treaties, and some of them didn't, and so on and so on. Two hundred and fifty years of it, and we have hardly touched it in the Western, in my opinion" ("The Western," The Governor's Sesquicentennial Literary Conference). As part of what has been successfully touched, he cites Willa Cather's *Death Comes for the Archbishop* and other such works.

Capps's affection for books is especially deep for those that contain information he uses to provide background for his writing. These are too numerous to list, but Capps observes a principle followed by writers, especially those who include historical data in their work. He says that writers will have a collection of books to which they turn for resource material. They may not know the books by title or even perhaps by author, but they will know a certain book and what kind of information is available there. Of his research, Capps said in an interview, "I find research interesting. It is not a task. If you are interested enough in something to write about it, and a novel is a heck of a lot of work to me, you don't mind doing the work. I have to be dedicated to a book to work that hard on it. Therefore, researching into it as far as I can to see what really went on is part of the whole thing."

Capps is a successful researcher and is particularly skilled at adapting the material he uses. Lee says of the historical authenticity in Capps's novels: "He has few peers in the realistic rendering of a time and a place. A reader of a Benjamin Capps novel can be assured that the times depicted are accurate and that the places are minutely described. Capps creates a world of his own that no history of the period will belie" ("Benjamin Capps" in *Fifty Western Writers* 43). He does so by carefully selecting the material and incidents to include: "I have a dozen possibilities of details for action, character, and everything else for every three or four that I use. For that reason I think a writer can't do enough research. Of course, the research must stop sometime, but it can't stop until the writer really understands the feeling of the people in that time and in that place. If the writer feels uncertain about details of that time and place, the reader will find that out. But there will come a time when the writer won't worry about that, and then the story will sound authentic" (Interview). By doing his work well, Capps has, as Paul Crume notes, avoided "the trick of Western stories" (21) and has instead written fiction that can withstand serious examination.

Capps speaks positively about the quality of research materials available to writers about the West. These writers are concerned about activities that occurred only one hundred years ago, and the primary source materials are readily available to the researcher. He cites particularly such materials as copies of the actual letters that General William Tecumseh Sherman wrote to his battalion commanders at the Battle of the Rosebud and the commanders' responses. That material, available from the National Archives and other such places, is a gold mine for the novelist. Capps has done research in the Amon Carter Museum in Ft. Worth, Texas, in newspapers held there on microfilm. He says, "We do not have the possibility of finding out what happened in ancient Rome or Egypt, but we do about these things. It is possible to find out very accurate information." He goes on to note, however, that "some of those early editors were pretty free with the information and often gave a lot more impression than they did anything else" ("The Western," The Governor's Sesquicentennial Literary Conference).

Capps is not reluctant to talk also about how he works. One of the most frequently asked questions to writers—other than "How did you get your first book published?" or "How do I place my book?"—is "How do you write?" The belief seems to be that the successful writer has found a unique formula for producing quality work. The answer to the question varies with the writers of course, but Capps has addressed the subject in his usual direct manner. In a 1976 article by Robert Hart in the *Grand Prairie Urbanite,* Capps says, "I have to get where I am not involved with people, where I don't have to answer the door bell. I have to feel that I have time. I don't like to be rushed and for that reason I wouldn't have made much of a newspaperman" (1). Capps's routine has been rigorous. He has tried to work an eight-hour day, which may include writing as well as working on his notes and reading. At the Governor's Sesquicentennial Literary Conference, Capps provided several insightful observations on the subject of how he writes. He said that one of the ways he organizes and sequences his material is to tape manila folders together to make an accordion file. Then he puts notes in the appropriate folder, each one representing a different chapter in the book. As a variant method, he has thumbtacked materials to the wall, and in this way he can visually place individual actions in the story in the proper order. His method of composition, like that of Mark Twain, is to compose in bed, leaning on his left elbow and writing with his right hand. He writes the material in spiral notebooks on the right side and uses the left side for additions or alterations. Then he types a draft of the work. He usually works through two typewritten drafts of each work, so a considerable amount of rewriting goes into the effort. For this he still uses a "modern" typewriter he bought in 1946. He has not made the conversion to the word processor.

Capps's ambition in writing "is to write clearly and simply and straightforwardly as the subject matter will permit" (Commire 30). By living a conservative, even frugal personal lifestyle, Capps has managed to make a living and, more important, to write what he wanted to write and not be dictated to by New York editors. Sonnichsen notes in the "Afterword" to *The Brothers of Uterica* that "above all, [Capps] wanted to understand what went on a century ago—not to accuse, not to justify, just to show how things really were. He would have to deal with violence, but he would not pour on the gore. He would have to handle sex, but there would be no perversion, no explicit scenes, no youths copulating with animals out in the barn. His people would talk the way people talked, but there would be no over use of the Anglo-Saxon monosyllables" (311). Sonnichsen is correct. For example, Capps related this story in an interview: When one editor suggested that Capps include explicit sex in one of his books, Capps told the editor that he did not know anything about explicit sex. Hence, he should not try to write about such matters.

Capps has not been particularly fond of critics or scholars because many have tended to belittle or deny the validity of the western experience in literature, particularly as it usually appears in the formula Western. In his three-part article "The Promise of Western Fiction," he assaults some of the critics. He says that they "write criticism and make pronouncements about literature [that] do not . . . enlighten or inform . . . but . . . cover up their own blindness and limitations as writers. They speak with arrogant authority, without good sense. Their ideas are encoded and enshrined and their perverted influence goes on" (Part 1, 1). In Part 1 of this essay he explores the problem facing the writer of the serious Western. He characterizes this problem as the same as that of any other American writer, "to probe the depths of his material, to understand it, to find what is inspiring in it, to believe in its worthiness, to respect it. In order to do these things he must free himself from certain inhibiting critical ideas that are pervasive and perverse, and when he has done so, maybe he will produce fiction which will cause a bunch of critics to also free themselves from the same stupid ideas" (1). He goes on to note, "If some of the scholars who have been analyzing Western fiction and gleefully pronouncing it all myth would get off that kick and, instead, get busy finding out what did happen, it would be a blessing." He also presents questions that could be productively explored: "Was there a West? Were millions of people involved in it? Was it almost like a laboratory for the study of the moving and mingling of greatly various people? Did significant patterns lie behind all that happened? Did the Westering experience strongly affect the nature of what is now the most interesting and important nation on earth?" His answer is strongly in the affirmative, as all his works clearly demonstrate. "The important thing for the western writer . . . is not to allow a critical climate to give him an inferiority complex. If he wants to write a potboiler, let him do it for the perfectly good reason that he deserves a full pot as much as the next fellow, and not for the false reason that Western subject matter is good for nothing else" ("Part 3" 24).

Capps has strong feelings about the value of the art form and subject matter to which he has devoted his life. In the same article he writes that the western experience was "so dramatic and intricate and little explained, so compelling as to almost demand a myth." He makes his point by noting, "Why is it that writers cannot leave the Custer affair alone? . . . For the same reason that the classic Greeks couldn't leave alone the family of Atreus or the royal house of Thebes" ("Part 3," 24). In his review of John Erickson's *The Hunter,* a retelling in nineteenth-century West Texas of the Gilgamesh epic, Capps says, "There is certainly room in the West of the 19th Century to tell or to retell the universal profound legends of human beings" (4L). Capps extends this idea in his review of *Corey Lane,* a novel by Norman Zollinger, which retells as a Western the story of the Roman Coriolanus, the subject of work by Plutarch as well as by Shakespeare. Zollinger's plot deals with the sheriff of a western town who tries to join the Apache War Chief, Victorio, and is killed after having turned against both his town and his enemies-turned-ally. Capps applauds the notion of using this classic story although he is not too pleased with Zollinger's handling of the material, which he feels is manipulative (n.p.). To further emphasize this point,

Capps says in a memorial article on Dorothy M. Johnson that she did not manipulate the reader but "merely provided the meaningful persuasive details knowing that all thoughtful readers have similar responses if they believe what they are reading. One has to be very human and believe in the humanity of others to write as she did" ("An Appreciation" 4).

Of the Western, he has said in an interview, "I think many serious Westerns have a psychological impact. Human beings have a common thread that runs through humanity so that possibilities always exist for a serious work. I believe the Western is growing up. I look forward to a lot of Westerns that are the best literature." Also in his memorial article on Dorothy M. Johnson he says "it seems to me it's time for writers whose roots are in the West to assert themselves and quit bowing to the provincialism of other places and times. . . . [These writers must] quit saying that someone was a good western writer or even saying a good American writer" ("An Appreciation" 4). His view is strong, as Stowers quotes him: "The more I get into it, the more certain I am that there are amazing possibilities in western writing for anyone who will respect [the writer's] material" ("Benjamin Capps" 25). He also feels that "when the Great American Novel is written, it will . . . be a western" ("The Promise of Western Fiction, 3" 24) because the setting embodies the unique flavor of American life better than any other possibly can.

CONCLUSION

The contribution of Benjamin Capps to the overall discussion of life in the American West is admittedly small if one compares his output to that of a popularizer such as Louis L'Amour. Even when compared with the work of fellow serious western writer Elmer Kelton, whose best work invites comparison, Capps's output seems small. Kelton has written twenty-eight novels, more than twice as many as Capps, but only six of Kelton's are serious novels; the others are by Kelton's own admission in the popular vein and are much like Capps's one formula Western, *Hanging at Comanche Wells*. But if one evaluates Capps on the quality, not the quantity, of his output, there is no question that he is one of the major writers about the American West.

Capps has written what is by common consent a superior trail drive novel in *The Trail to Ogallala* and has presented outstanding character studies of frontiersmen in *Sam Chance* and *The True Memoirs of Charley Blankenship*. He has dealt with a small but significant element of Texas life in *The Brothers of Uterica.* He has been bold enough to try the contemporary novel set in the West in *The Heirs of Franklin Woodstock,* bringing his range from the frontier to the present. Perhaps his most significant work, however, has been with the plight of the Indians in *The White Man's Road, A Woman of the People,* and *Woman Chief.* In all, his fiction will likely be remembered as his most significant accomplishment, but one cannot overlook his historical work, especially *The Warren Wagontrain Raid.* In it, Capps reveals his ability to tell a factual, documented story in a narrative so smooth that historians have been troubled by its storylike approach and the imagined thoughts and conversations of its people. No one can argue that *The Great Chiefs* and *The Indians* are important new contributions to historical research and writing. But these volumes put accurate, interesting material into the hands of countless thousands throughout the world and have set to rest some of the erroneous ideas—myths, if they must be so called—and replaced them with facts.

Capps's work entitles him to belong to the ranks of the very best writers. He says that he would like to be remembered "as an author who wrote about human nature, human relationship" (Interview). In an interview with Bob St. John, Capps admitted that he is not "particularly in the mainstream of the popular style of writing today" (3D). But the label of "regionalist" so casually applied to anyone who pursues the subjects Capps has found attractive does not fit Capps and may well prevent him from getting the credit and critical acclaim he so richly deserves. Perhaps the slow stream of critical articles thus far will swell as scholars examine Capps's work for its content and style. But the whole field of study of western American literature has come of age since the beginning of this decade, particularly through works such as Erisman and Etulain's *Fifty Western Writers* and the massive *A Literary History of the American West,* as well as the continual surge of pamphlets in the Western Writer Series from Boise State University. All of these are positive indicators of the coming of age of a body of material usually shunted aside as a casual concern for cowboys and Indians. Capps may be correct in his belief that the Great American Novel will be a Western. He says, "Few other areas of experience in North America speak so clearly to the basic fabric of the American people, good or bad, and recently enough to be well documented in archival records" (Interview). The material includes the independent spirit of the frontier, the Anglo desire to dominate the land and its people for good or ill, the personalities and events that draw admiration and arouse emotion, and the great expanse of the Plains of the central portion and the forests of the far West. Here, in this mixing and clashing of cultures, the American experience can be drawn out from the experience of the Indian, black, Hispanic, European, Asian immigrant, and Anglo. As Capps has said, the material affords so much for the fiction writer that it cannot be ignored.

SELECTED BIBLIOGRAPHY

PRIMARY SOURCES

NOVELS BY BENJAMIN CAPPS

The Brothers of Uterica. New York: Meredith Press, 1967; reprint, New York: Popular Library, n.d.; reprint, Dallas: Southern Methodist UP, 1988.

Hanging at Comanche Wells. New York: Ballantine Books, 1962.

The Heirs of Franklin Woodstock. Fort Worth: Texas Christian UP, 1989.

Sam Chance. New York: Duell, Sloan and Pearce, 1965; reprint, New York: New American Library, 1965; Dallas: Southern Methodist UP, 1987.

The Trail to Ogallala. New York: Duell, Sloan and Pearce, 1964; reprint, New York: New American Library, 1965; New York: Ace Books, n.d.; Fort Worth: Texas Christian UP, 1985.

The True Memoirs of Charley Blankenship. Philadelphia: J.B. Lippincott, 1972.

The White Man's Road. New York: Harper and Row, 1969; reprint, New York: Ace Books, n.d.; reprint, Dallas: Southern Methodist UP, 1988.

Woman Chief. Garden City, New York: Doubleday, 1979; reprint, New York: Ace Books, forthcoming.

A Woman of the People. New York: Duell, Sloan and Pearce, 1966; reprint, Greenwich, Connecticut: Fawcett, n.d.; Albuquerque: New Mexico UP, 1985.

NONFICTION BOOKS BY BENJAMIN CAPPS

The Great Chiefs. New York: Time-Life Books, 1975.

The Indians. New York: Time-Life Books, 1973.

The Warren Wagontrain Raid, The First Complete Account of an Historic Indian Attack and Its Aftermath. New York: Dial, 1974; reprint, Dallas: Southern Methodist UP, 1989.

EDITED BY BENJAMIN CAPPS

Duncan Robinson: Texas Teacher and Humanist. Eds. Benjamin Capps and Thomas Sutherland. Arlington: Texas at Arlington UP (English Department), 1976.

ARTICLES, STORIES, AND OTHER WORK BY BENJAMIN CAPPS

"Apologia." *The Warren Wagontrain Raid,* by Benjamin Capps. Dallas: Southern Methodist UP, 1989: xiii–xviii.

"An Appreciation: Dorothy M. Johnson." *The Roundup* 33.2 (1985): 4–5.

"Blind Man's Bluff." *Texas Literary Quarterly* 1 (1949): 39–42.

"Brands." *Lariat Story Magazine* (data unavailable).

"Breaking into Print." *The Roundup* 21.4 (1973): 1–2.

"Buckner's Reef." (No data available).

"Building Tanks for Stock Raised Appreciation for Clean Water." *Dallas Times Herald* 2 October 1983: 36A.

"Centennial!" *Texas, Our Texas: 150 Moments That Made Us the Way We Are*. Austin: Texas Monthly Press, 1986: 151.

"Chief Tragedy of Indians—Plague—Seldom Recounted." *Fort Worth Star-Telegram* 4 July 1976: 1, 6H.

"Cimarron, The Killer." *Westward Magazine: Dallas Times Herald* 6 February 1983: 4–6.

"A Critical Look at a Classic Western Novel." *The Roundup* 22.6 (1964): 2, 4.

"The Disgraceful Affair of Turpentine Jackson." In *The Roundup,* ed. Stephen Overholser. Garden City, New York: Doubleday, 1982: 52–57.

"Eating Well in Lean Times." *Dallas Times Herald* 2 September 1982: 38A.

Introduction. *Fodor's Southwest*. Eds. Robert C. Fisher and Leslie Brown. New York: David McKay, 1979: 1–8.

Introduction. *Fodor's South Central States*. Eds. Eugene Fodor, Robert C. Fisher, and Barnett D. Laschever. New York: David McKay, 1966: 11–18.

"Kid Curry and the Wild Bunch." *Lariat Story Magazine*. July 1949: 31–36.

"The Last Bearden." *Alfred Hitchcock's Mystery Magazine*. December 1963: 64–72.

"Law Comes to the Old West: Do-It-Yourself Justice." *Fodor's Old West: A Practical Guide to Where the West Was Won*. Eds. Eugene Fodor and Robert C. Fisher. New York: David McKay, 1976: 78–92.

Letter to Ernest Speck. 20 August 1973.

Letter to Ernest Speck. 1 September 1974.

Letter to Ernest Speck. 6 March 1978.

Letter to Ernest Speck. 21 July 1981.

Letter to Mody Boatright. 23 March 1964.

Letter to Mody Boatright. 12 July 1965.

Letter to Lawrence Clayton. 9 December 1988.

Letter to Lawrence Clayton. 27 February 1989.

Letter to James Ward Lee. 19 January 1984.

"Lifetime of Lessons: Pioneer Mother Was Teacher First, Foremost." *Dallas Times Herald* 21 October 1984: 44A.

"Mama, Bill, Roy & Me." *Westward Magazine: Dallas Times Herald* 20 December 1981: 13, 16–17.

"Memories Remain of Anarene." *Dallas Times Herald* 5 Sunday 1985: 41A.

"Overture to Ogallala." *The Roundup* 22.9 (1974): 1–2, 8.

"The Promise of Western Fiction, Part 1." *The Roundup* 17.10: 1–2, 20; Part 2, 17.11 (1969): 2, 4, 14; Part 3, 17.12 (1969): 6, 8, 24.

"The Second Best Navigator." *Texas Literary Quarterly* 1 (1948): 16–17, 31–33.

"A Secret of Military Significance." *Westward Magazine: Dallas Times Herald* 8 November 1981: 24–27.

"Slim Wilkinson." *Horsing Around: Contemporary Cowboy Humor.* Eds. Lawrence Clayton and Kenneth Davis. Detroit: Wayne State University Press, forthcoming.

"Tom Horn—Lawman and Renegade." *Lariat Story Magazine* (data unavailable).

"Uncle Rufus and the Cat-Scratch." *Sir!* December 1949: 48–49, 68–69.

"The Western." Address to the Governor's Sesquicentennial Literary Conference. Denton, Texas, 24–27 September 1986.

SELECTED BOOK REVIEWS BY BENJAMIN CAPPS

These entries demonstrate the range and extent of Capps's reviews. The list was developed from files of the reviews in the University of Texas at Arlington Special Collection and Capps's own files. Dates and page numbers are not indicated on many of the clipped items.

Abernethy, F.E., ed. *T for Texas: A State Full of Folklore. Dallas Times Herald* 26 December 1982: n.p.

—. *Legendary Ladies of Texas. Dallas Morning News* 27 September 1981: 4G.

Adams, Ramon F., and Bob Kinnon. *From the Pecos to the Powder: A Cowboy's Autobiography. Saturday Review* 22 May 1965: 84.

Arnold, Oren. *Irons in the Fire: Cattle Brand Lore. New York Times Book Review* 30 May 1965: 20–21.

Axford, Joseph "Mack." *Around Western Campfires. Fort Worth Star-Telegram* 18 May 1969: n.p.

Baker, Betty. *The Dunderhead War. Fort Worth Star-Telegram* n.d.: n.p.

Ballard, Todhunter, ed. *The Western Bonanza, Eight Short Novels of the West. Fort Worth Star-Telegram* 2 November 1969: n.p.

Barker, S. Omar. *Rawhide Rhymes. Fort Worth Star-Telegram* 8 December 1968: n.p.

Bean, Emilia. *Time of Outrage. Fort Worth Star-Telegram* 5 November 1967: n.p.

Berkhofer, Robert F. *The White Man's Indian. Fort Worth Star-Telegram* 30 April 1978: 9F.

Billington, Ray Allen. *America's Frontier Heritage. Fort Worth Star-Telegram* n.d.: n.p.

Blevins, Winfred. *Give Your Heart to the Hawks. Fort Worth Star-Telegram* 28 October 1973: n.p.

Bobo, Zack, Jr. *Ramblings of a Country Doctor. Fort Worth Star-Telegram* 16 October 1977: n.p.

Brophy, William, and Sophie Aberle, comps. *The Indian, America's Unfinished Business. Fort Worth Star-Telegram* 18 December 1966: n.p.

Bourke, John G. *On the Border with Crook. Fort Worth Star-Telegram* 14 December 1969: n.p.

Brand, Max. *Troubled Kid. Fort Worth Star-Telegram* 5 April 1970: n.p.

Brett, Bill. *The Stolen Steers. Fort Worth Star-Telegram* 22 May 1977: n.p.

Brown, J.P.S. *The Outfit. Fort Worth Star-Telegram* n.d.: n.p.

Brown, Mark H. *The Flight of the Nez Perce. Fort Worth Star-Telegram* 5 February 1967: n.p.

Brown, Tom, Jr., and William Jon Watkins. *The Tracker: The Story of Tom Brown, Jr. Fort Worth Star-Telegram* 12 November 1978: 8G.

Carter, Forrest. *Gone to Texas. Fort Worth Star-Telegram* 10 August 1975: 7H.

Chrisman, Harry E. *Fifty Years on the Owl Hoot Trail. Fort Worth Star-Telegram* 24 August 1969: n.p.

Clark, Ella E. *Indian Legends From the Northern Rockies. Fort Worth Star-Telegram* 7 August 1966: n.p.

Clarke, Mary Whatley. *A Century of Cow Business. Fort Worth Star-Telegram* 13 February 1977: n.p.

—. *The Slaughter Ranches and Their Makers. Dallas Morning News* 4 January 1981: n.p.

—. *The Swenson Saga and the SMS Ranches. Fort Worth Star-Telegram* 13 March 1977: n.p.

Crosby, Thelma, and Eve Ball. *Bob Crosby: World Cowboy*

Champion. Fort Worth Star-Telegram 25 December 1966: n.p.

Culp, John. *A Whistle in the Wind. Fort Worth Star-Telegram* 7 July 1968: n.p.

Curry, Jane Louise. *Down From the Lonely Mountain. New York Times* n.d.: n.p.

Danker, Donald. *Molly: The Journal of Molly Dorsey Sanford. Fort Worth Star-Telegram* 25 April 1976: 7H.

Debo, Angie. *Geronimo: The Man, His Time, His Place. Fort Worth Star-Telegram* 1 January 1978: n.p.

Decker, William. *To Be a Man. Fort Worth Star-Telegram* 2 March 1969: n.p.

Dillon, Richard. *Meriwether Lewis: A Biography. Saturday Review* 29 February 1965: 27; *Fort Worth Star-Telegram* 21 February 1965: n.p.

Drake, Laurie Nan. *The Long Road. Fort Worth Star-Telegram* 5 April 1970: n.p.

Eastman, Charles A. *Indian Boyhood. Fort Worth Star-Telegram* 20 February 1972: n.p.

Eby, Cecil. *That Disgraceful Affair, The Black Hawk War. Fort Worth Star-Telegram* 30 December 1973: 6F.

Elliott, David Stewart. *The Dalton Gang and the Coffeyville Raid. Fort Worth Star-Telegram* 11 August 1968: n.p.

Ellison, Glen R. "Slim". *Cowboys Under the Mogollon Rim. Fort Worth Star-Telegram* 8 December 1968: n.p.

Emmett, Chris. *Texas Camel Tales. Fort Worth Star-Telegram* 5 April 1970: n.p.

Erickson, John R. *The Hunter. Dallas Times Herald* 17 June 1984: 4L.

Evans, Max. *Shadow of Thunder. Fort Worth Star-Telegram* 29 June 1969: n.p.

Ewers, John C. *Indian Life on the Upper Missouri. Fort Worth Star-Telegram* 14 July 1968: n.p.

Faulk, Odie B. *Destiny Road: The Gila Trail and the Opening of the Southwest. Fort Worth Star-Telegram* 21 October 1973: n.p.

Fisher, O.C., and J.C. Dykes. *King Fisher: His Life and Times. Fort Worth Star-Telegram* 20 November 1966: n.p.

Fodor, Eugene, ed. *Fodor-Shell Travel Guides, U.S.A. Fort Worth Star-Telegram* 5 June 1966: n.p.

Folsom, James K. *The American Western Novel. Fort Worth Star-Telegram* 25 September 1966: n.p.

Foreman, Paul. *Quanah. Dallas Morning News* 17 July 1983: n.p.

Fulton, Maurice. *History of the Lincoln County War. Fort Worth Star-Telegram* 13 October 1968: n.p.

Gaillardet, Frederic. *Sketches of Early Texas and Louisiana. Fort Worth Star-Telegram* 12 February 1967: n.p.

Gard, Wayne. *Sam Bass. Fort Worth Star-Telegram* 8 December 1968: n.p.; *Dallas Times Herald* 6 April 1969: n.p.

Gilbert, Bill. *The Westering Man: The Life of Joseph Walker. Dallas Morning News* n.d.: n.p.

Graff, Stuart, and Polly Graff. *Squanto, Indian Adventurer. New York Times* 30 May 1965: 20.

Greenberg, Alvin. *The Invention of the West. Fort Worth Star-Telegram* 3 April 1977: n.p.

Greenberg, David B., ed. *Land That Our Fathers Plowed. Fort Worth Star-Telegram* 29 June 1969: n.p.

Grove, Fred. *Buffalo Runners. Fort Worth Star-Telegram* 8 December 1968: n.p.

Guerin, Elsa Jane. *Mountain Charlie or the Adventures of Mrs. E.J. Guerin. Fort Worth Star-Telegram* 1 September 1968: n.p.

Guthrie, A.B., Jr. *The Blue Hen's Chick: A Life in Context. Fort Worth Star-Telegram* 9 May 1965: n.p.

Haines, Francis. *The Plains Indians. Fort Worth Star-Telegram* 25 April 1976: 7H.

Haley, James. *The Buffalo War. Fort Worth Star-Telegram* 25 April 1976: 7H.

Hall, B.C. *Keepers of the Feast. Dallas Morning News* 19 October 1980: n.p.

Hamric, Roy, ed. *Archer Fullingim: A Country Editor's View of Life. Fort Worth Star-Telegram* 9 November 1975: n.p.

Harman, Fred. *The Great West in Paintings. Fort Worth Star-Telegram* 2 November 1969: n.p.

Haynes, Glynn W. *The American Paint Horse*. *Fort Worth Star-Telegram* n.d.: n.p.

Harris, Christie. *West With the White Chiefs*. *New York Times Book Review* 4 April 1965: n.p.

Heard, John Norman. *The Black Frontiersmen*. *Fort Worth Star-Telegram* 23 June 1968: n.p.

Hedgpeth, Don. *The Texas Breed: A Cowboy Anthology*. *Fort Worth Star-Telegram* 22 October 1978: n.p.

Heiderstadt, Dorothy. *Marie Tanglehair*. *New York Times Book Review* 30 May 1965: 21.

Henry, Will. *Alias, Butch Cassidy*. *Fort Worth Star-Telegram* 28 January 1968: n.p.

—. *I, Tom Horn*. *Fort Worth Star-Telegram* n.d.: n.p.

Hill, Ruth Beebe. *Hanta Yo*. *Fort Worth Star-Telegram* 4 March 1974: 10G.

Hine, Robert V. *Community on the American Frontier*. *Dallas Morning News* 22 March 1981: 5G.

Hoffman, Lee. *West of Cheyenne*. *Fort Worth Star-Telegram* 2 March 1969: n.p.

Hoffsinde, Robert. *Indian Warriors and Their Weapons*. *New York Times Book Review* 30 March 1965: 20.

Hoig, Stan. *Humor of the American Cowboy*. *Fort Worth Star-Telegram* 31 May 1970: 7F.

Holloway, Mark. *Heavens on Earth*. *Fort Worth Star-Telegram* 30 October 1966: n.p.

Holm, Don. *Old-Fashioned Dutch Oven Cookbook*. *Fort Worth Star-Telegram* 14 December 1969: n.p.

Humphrey, William. *My Moby Dick. Fort Worth Star-Telegram* 12 November 1979: 8G.

Hunter, Evan. *The Chisholms. Fort Worth Star-Telegram* 26 September 1976: 7G.

Inman, Col. Henry. *Buffalo Jones' Adventures on the Plains. Fort Worth Star-Telegram* 31 May 1970: 7F.

Jahoda, Gloria. *The Trail of Tears. Fort Worth Star-Telegram* 29 February 1976: 7H.

Johnson, Dorothy M. *The Bloody Bozeman. Fort Worth Star-Telegram* n.d.: n.p.

—. *Buffalo Woman. Fort Worth Star-Telegram* n.d.: n.p.

—. *Flame on the Frontier: Short Stories by Pioneer Women. Western American Literature* 2 (1968): 304–05; *Fort Worth Star-Telegram* 25 June 1967: n.p.

Johnson, Virginia Weise. *The Long, Long Trail: A Reminiscence. Fort Worth Star-Telegram* 19 June 1966: n.p.

Jones, Douglas C. *Arrest Sitting Bull. Fort Worth Star-Telegram* 11 December 1977: n.p.

—. *A Creek Called Wounded Knee. Fort Worth Star-Telegram* 3 December 1978: n.p.

—. *The Treaty of Medicine Lodge. Fort Worth Star-Telegram* 13 November 1966: n.p.

Jones, James. *From Here to Eternity. Tahlequah Star-Citizen* 28 June 1951: magazine section, n.p.

Kelton, Elmer. *The Day the Cowboys Quit. Fort Worth Star-Telegram* n.d.: n.p.

—. *The Good Old Boys. Fort Worth Star-Telegram* 14 May 1978: 9F.

Kemp, Ben W., and J.C. Dykes. *Cow Dust and Saddle Leather. Fort Worth Star-Telegram* n.d.: n.p.

Knaggs, John R. *The Bugles Are Silent: A Novel of the Texan Revolution. Fort Worth Star-Telegram* 26 February 1978: n.p.

Lancaster, Richard. *Piegan. Fort Worth Star-Telegram* 28 August 1966: n.p.

Latorre, Felipe, and Delores Latorre. *The Mexican Kickapoo Indians. Fort Worth Star-Telegram* 29 February 1976: 7H.

Lee, Mabel Barbe. *Back in Cripple Creek. Fort Worth Star-Telegram* n.d.: n.p.

Leekley, Thomas. *The World of Manabozho. New York Times* n.d.: n.p.

Maddox, Web. *Black Sheep. Fort Worth Star-Telegram* 27 July 1975: n.p.

Marriott, Alice. *Indian Annie: Kiowa Captive. New York Times Book Review* 30 May 1965: 21.

McLean, Malcolm D., ed. *Papers Concerning Robetson's Colony in Texas, vol. 9. Dallas Times Herald* 12 December 1982: 5L.; *Dallas Morning News* 6 December 1981: 4G.

McLuhan, T.C., comp. *Touch the Earth. Fort Worth Star-Telegram* 20 February 1972: n.p.

Meade, Richard. *Big Bend. Fort Worth Star-Telegram* 13 October 1968: n.p.

Meadowcroft, Enid La Monte. *Crazy Horse, Sioux Warrior. New York Times Book Review* 30 May 1965: 20.

Merriam, H.G., ed. *Way Out West: Recollections and Tales. Fort Worth Star-Telegram* 29 June 1969: n.p.

Metz, Leon. *John Selman, Texas Gunfighter. Fort Worth Star-Telegram* n.d.: n.p.

Moody, Ralph. *Horse of a Different Color, Reminiscences of a Kansas Drover. Fort Worth Star-Telegram* 13 October 1968: n.p.

Moore, Daniel G. *Log of a Twentieth Century Cowboy. Saturday Review* 25 May 1965: 84.

—. *Enter Without Knocking. Fort Worth Star-Telegram* 2 March 1969: n.p.

Moorhead, Max L. *The Apache Frontier: Jacobo Ugarte and the Spanish-Indian Relations in Northern New Spain. Fort Worth Star-Telegram* 11 August 1968: n.p.

Myres, S.D., ed. *Pioneer Surveyor–Frontier Lawyer: The Personal Narrative of O.W. Williams, 1877–1902. Western American Literature* 1 (1967): 311–12.

Nabokov, Peter. *Two Leggings: The Making of a Crow Warrior. Fort Worth Star-Telegram* 16 July 1967: n.p.

Neihardt, John G. *The Mountain Men. Fort Worth Star-Telegram* n.d.: n.p.

Nordhoff, Charles. *Communistic Societies of the United States. Fort Worth Star-Telegram* 30 October 1966: n.p.

Noyes, John Humphrey. *History of American Socialisms. Fort Worth Star-Telegram* 30 October 1966: n.p.

O'Conner, Jack. *Horses and Buggy West. Fort Worth Star-Telegram* 8 December 1968: n.p.; *Dallas Times Herald* 6 April 1969: n.p.

Parker, William Thornton. *Animals of Old Fort Cummings, New Mexico, 1867–1868. Fort Worth Star-Telegram* 11 August 1968: n.p.

Patterson, Paul. *Crazy Women in the Rafters. Fort Worth Star-Telegram* n.d.: n.p.

Payne, Darwin. *Dallas: An Illustrated History. Times Herald Extra—East* 26 January 1983: 2A.

Price, Eugene H. *Open Range Ranching on the South Plains in the 1890's. Fort Worth Star-Telegram* 10 September 1967: n.p.

Randolph, Edmund. *Beef, Leather, and Grass. Dallas Morning News* 22 March 1981: 5G.

Rascoe, Jesse. *Southern California Treasures. Fort Worth Star-Telegram* 18 May 1969: n.p.

Ray, Ophelia. *Daughter of the Tejas. New York Times.* 30 May 1965: 20.

Reese, John. *Sun Blind Range. Fort Worth Star-Telegram* 13 October 1968: n.p.

Richardson, Boyce. *Strangers Devour the Land. Fort Worth Star-Telegram* 29 February 1975: 7H.

Rickards, Colon. *Mysterious Dave Mather. Fort Worth Star-Telegram* 11 August 1968: n.p.

Roach, Joyce. *The Cowgirls. Fort Worth Star-Telegram* 5 March 1978: n.p.

Sanders, Leonard, and Ronnie C. Tyler. *How Fort Worth*

Became the Texasmost City. Fort Worth Star-Telegram 27 January 1974: n.p.

Sandoz, Mari. *The Battle of the Little Bighorn. Fort Worth Star-Telegram* 26 June 1966: n.p.

Schaefer, Jack. *Heroes Without Glory. Fort Worth Star-Telegram* 18 April 1965: n.p.

Schoenberger, Dale T. *The Gunfighters. Fort Worth Star-Telegram* 20 February 1972: n.p.

Schueler, Donald G. *Incident at Eagle Ranch. Dallas Morning News* n.d.: n.p.

Sekaquaptewa, Helen, with Louise Udall. *Me and Mine, The Life Story of Helen Sekaquaptewa. Fort Worth Star-Telegram* 8 December 1968: n.p.; *Dallas Times Herald* 6 April 1969: n.p.

Shelley, John, and David Shelley. *Hell-for-Leather Jones. Fort Worth Star-Telegram* 2 March 1969: n.p.

Sierra Club. "Wilderness Calendar for 1969." *Fort Worth Star-Telegram* 8 December 1968: n.p.

Silverberg, Robert. *The Old Ones. New York Times* 30 May 1965: 20.

Simms, Orland. *Cowpokes, Nesters, and So Forth. Fort Worth Star-Telegram* 4 April 1971: 7G.

Smith, George Alan, and Carol D. Smith. "The Armchair Mountaineer." *Western American Literature* 5 (1971): 160–61.

Smith, H. Alan. *The Great Chili Confrontation. Fort Worth Star-Telegram* n.d.: n.p.

Smith, Rex Alan. *Moon of Popping Trees. Fort Worth Star-Telegram* 28 December 1975: 7F.

Sonnichsen, C.L. *Colonel Greene and the Copper Skyrocket. Fort Worth Star-Telegram* n.d.: n.p.

Spencer, Alma Dill Russell. *Green Russell and Gold. Fort Worth Star-Telegram* 8 January 1967: n.p.

Stands in Timber, John, and Margot Liberty. *Cheyenne Memories. Western American Literature* 3 (1968): 164–65.

Steckmesser, Kent Lad. *The Western Hero in History in Legend. Fort Worth Star-Telegram* 25 April 1965: n.p.

Stegner, Wallace. *Angle of Repose. Fort Worth Star-Telegram* 4 April 1971: 7G.

Steiner, Stan. *The Ranchers: A Book of Generations. Dallas Morning News* 4 January 1981: n.p.

Strong, W.E. *A Trip to the Yellowstone National Park in July, August, and September of 1875. Fort Worth Star-Telegram* n.d.: n.p.

Stroud, Harry. *Conquest of the Prairies. Fort Worth Star-Telegram* 11 August 1968: n.p.

Sutton, Felix. *North American Indians. New York Times Book Review* n.d.: n.p.

Tatum, Lawrie. *Our Red Brothers and the Peace Policy of President Ulysses S. Grant. Fort Worth Star-Telegram* 31 May 1970: 7F.

Taylor, J. Golden. *The Literature of the American West. Fort Worth Star-Telegram* 4 April 1971: 7G.

Thompson, Hildegard. *American Indians Today. New York Times Book Review* 30 May 1965: 20.

Townshend, R.B. *A Tenderfoot in Colorado. Fort Worth Star-Telegram* 1 September 1968: n.p.

Turner, Elsa McFarland. *Look High, Grow Tall. Fort Worth Star-Telegram* 10 September 1967: n.p.

Turner, Frederick Jackson. *America's Great Frontiers and Sections,* ed. Wilbur R. Jacobs. *Fort Worth Star-Telegram* 24 August 1969: n.p.

Turner, William O. *Mayberly's Kill. Fort Worth Star-Telegram* 18 May 1969: n.p.

Ulyatt, Kenneth. *North Against the Sioux. Fort Worth Star-Telegram* n.d.: n.p.

Upton, Richard. *The Custer Adventure. Fort Worth Star-Telegram* 29 February 1976: 7H.

Van Cleve, Spike. *40 Years' Gatherin's. Fort Worth Star-Telegram* n.d.: n.p.

Vernam, Glen R. *Indian Hater. Fort Worth Star-Telegram* 24 August 1969: n.p.

Vestal, Stanley. *Jim Bridger, Mountain Man. Fort Worth Star-Telegram* 31 May 1970: 7F.

Walton, George. *Fearless and Free: The Seminole Indian War, 1835–1842. Fort Worth Star-Telegram* 15 January 1978: n.p.

Ware, Clyde. *The Innocents. Fort Worth Star-Telegram* 14 December 1969: n.p.; *Western American Literature* V (1971): 161–62.

Waters, Frank. *Pumpkin Seed Point. Fort Worth Star-Telegram* 18 May 1969: n.p.

Western Literature Association. *The Literary History of the American West. Texas Books in Review* September 1987: 8.

Wheeler, Sessions H. *Paiute. New York Times Book Review* 30 May 1965: 30.

Williams, Clayton. *Never Again: A History of Texas in Three Volumes. Fort Worth Star-Telegram* 2 November 1969: n.p.

Winsor, Kathleen. *Wanderers Eastward, Wanderers West. Saturday Review* 1 May 1965: 41; *Fort Worth Star-Telegram* 2 May 1965: n.p.

Wise, Jennings. *The Red Man in the New World Drama. Fort Worth Star-Telegram* 20 February 1972: n.p.

Woolley, Bryan. *Sam Bass. Dallas Times Herald* 6 November 1983: 4K.

Yava, Albert. *Big Falling Snow. Fort Worth Star-Telegram* 12 November 1978: 8G.

Yost, Karl, and Frederic G. Renner, comps. *A Bibliography of the Published Works of Charles M. Russell. Fort Worth Star-Telegram* 20 February 1972: n.p.

Yost, Nellie Snyder. *Boss Cowman: The Recollections of Ed Lemmon 1857–1946. Fort Worth Star-Telegram* n.d.: n.p.

Zollinger, Norman. *Corey Lane. Dallas Morning News* 24 January 1982: n.p.

SECONDARY SOURCES

Ball, Eve. *In the Days of Victorio: Recollections of a Warm Springs Apache*. Tuscon: Arizona UP, 1970.

Barnett, Joanna. "Critical Analysis of Benjamin Capps' *The White Man's Road*." Unpublished manuscript (based on interviews with Capps), Hardin-Simmons University, 1978.

Bellinghausen, Darlene. "A Brief Survey of Frederick Manfred's *Conquering Horse*." Unpublished manuscript, Hardin-Simmons University, 1989.

Bucco, Martin. Rev. of *The Brothers of Uterica,* by Benjamin Capps. *Western American Literature* 3 (1969): 308–10.

Commire, Anne. *Something about the Author*. Detroit: Gale, 1976.

Crume, Paul. "The West of Benjamin Capps." *Southwest Scene* (*Dallas Morning News* magazine) 24 January 1971: 18–22.

Decker, Williams. Rev. of *The White Man's Road,* by Benjamin Capps. *Saturday Review of Literature* 17 January 1970: 42.

Denig, Edwin Thompson. "Of the Crow Nation." *Anthropological Papers,* Number 33–42. Ed. John C. Ewers. *Bureau of American Ethnology Bulletin 151*. Washington, D.C., U.S. Government Printing Office, 1953: 64–68.

Dunkelberg, Lee. "Writer Covers South Plains." *Dallas Morning News* 26 January 1976: 1D.

Etulain, Richard W. Rev. of *The Brothers of Uterica,* by Benjamin Capps. *Journal of the West* 8 (1969): 656.

—. "The White Man's Road: An Appreciation." *Southwestern American Literature* 1 (1971): 88–92.

Fehrenbach, T.R. *Comanches: The Destruction of a People.* New York: Knopf, 1974.

Gard, Wayne. Rev. of *The Warren Wagontrain Raid,* by Benjamin Capps. *Southwestern Historical Quarterly* 78 (1974): 102–03.

Garfield, Brian. "Compassion for the Comanche." *Saturday Review* 19 March 1966: 39–40.

Graham, Don. "Old and New Cowboy Classics." *Southwest Review* 65 (1980): 293–303.

Gulinger, Ed. "Gaps Exist for Indians." *Grand Prairie Urbanite* 2 October 1969: 1.

Hart, Robert. "Capps Spurs Western Image." *Grand Prairie Urbanite* 19 May 1976: 1.

Kelton, Elmer. Afterword. *Sam Chance,* by Benjamin Capps. Dallas: Southern Methodist UP, 1987: 263–67.

—. "The Western and the Literary Ghetto." *Texas Literary Tradition,* ed. Don Graham, et al. Austin: The University of Texas (College of Arts and Sciences), 1983: 82–94.

Landsman, Neil. "Western Author Sets the Record Straight." *Grand Prairie Daily News* 31 December 1976: 1.

Leckie, William H. Rev. of *The Warren Wagontrain Raid,*

by Benjamin Capps. *The Western Historical Quarterly* 6 (1975): 187–88.

Lee, James Ward. Afterword. *The White Man's Road,* by Benjamin Capps. Dallas: Southern Methodist UP, 1988: 311–16.

—. Afterword. *A Woman of the People,* by Benjamin Capps. Albuquerque: New Mexico UP, 1985: 243–47.

—. "Benjamin Capps." *Fifty Western Writers,* eds. Fred Erisman and Richard Etulain. Westport, Connecticut: Greenwood 1982: 43.

—. "Benjamin Capps." *A Literary History of the American West.* Fort Worth: Texas Christian UP, 1986: 597–603.

—. *Classics of Texas Fiction.* Dallas: E-Heart, 1987.

Marr, Philip L. "The White Man's Road." *The Library Journal* 94 (1969): 2952.

Morgan, Edmund. Introduction. *The Founding of Massachusetts: Historians and the Sources.* New York: Bobbs Merrill, 1964: i–v.

Newcomb, W.W. *The Indians of Texas from Prehistoric to Modern Times.* Austin: Texas UP, 1961.

Pilkington, William T. "The Recent Southwestern Novel." *Southwestern American Literature* 1 (1971): 12–15.

Poulson, Richard C. "The Trail Drive Novel: A Matter of Balance." *Southwestern American Literature* 4 (1974): 53–61.

Richardson, Rupert N. *The Comanche Barrier to South*

Plains Settlement. Glendale, California: The Arthur A. Clark Co., 1933.

Rodenberger, Lou. "The 'Gen-u-wine Stuff': Character Makes the Difference in Trail-Drivin' Novel." *Heritage of Kansas* 11 (1978): 3–12.

—. "The Novel of the Cowboy." *Literary History of the American West,* ed. Thomas J. Lyon, et al. Fort Worth: Texas Christian UP, 1986: 523–33.

—. Review of *Sam Chance, The Brothers of Uterica,* and *The White Man's Road,* by Benjamin Capps. *Western American Literature* 24 (1989): 262–64.

Roripaugh, Robert A. Rev. of *A Woman of the People,* by Benjamin Capps. *Western American Literature* 2 (1967): 65–66.

Sanders, Leonard. "Capps' Novel Even Better." *Fort Worth Star-Telegram* 5 November 1967: 6G.

—. "Mid Passage Still Risky." *Fort Worth Star-Telegram* 30 September 1973: 6F.

Schneider, Jack. Rev. of *Woman Chief,* by Benjamin Capps. *Western American Literature* 15 (1980): 57–58.

Simpson, Mary. "Benjamin Capps and the Sacajawea Plagiarism Case." Unpublished master's thesis, North Texas State University, 1986.

Smith, C.W. "Novelist of the Frontier." *Sunday* (*Dallas Times Herald* magazine) 2 March 1980: 4–9.

Smith, Ralph A. "The Comanche Sun over Mexico." *West Texas Historical Association Year Book* 46 (1970): 25–62.

Sonnichsen, C.L. Afterword. *The Brothers of Uterica*, by Benjamin Capps. Dallas: Southern Methodist UP, 1989: 311–14.

—. *From Hopalong to Hud: Thoughts on Western Fiction*. College Station: Texas A&M UP, 1978.

—. "The New Style Western." *South Dakota Review* 4 (1966): 22–28.

—. Rev. of *The Warren Wagontrain Raid*, by Benjamin Capps. *Western American Literature* 9 (1974): 60–61.

—. Rev. of *The White Man's Road*, by Benjamin Capps. *Western American Literature* 4 (1970): 304–05.

Speck, Ernest B. *Benjamin Capps*. Western Writer Series. Boise: Boise State University, 1981.

—. Rev. of *The True Memoirs of Charley Blankenship*, by Benjamin Capps. *Southwestern American Literature* 2 (1972): 150–52.

St. John, Bob. "For Writer, No Showdown." *Dallas Morning News* 8 September 1978: 3D.

Stowers, Carlton. "Benjamin Capps. . . ." *Alcalde* January 1971: 23, 25.

—. "The Old West of Benjamin Capps." *Southwestern American Literature* 2 (1972): 150–52.

Taylor, Joe. "Ben Capps . . . He Tells about the West Like It Really Was." *Sunday* (*Dallas Times Herald* magazine) 3 June 1973: 18–19.

Tucker, Chris. "Western Novelist Ben Capps Writing on

the Range." *Dallas Morning News* 15 February 1981: 5G.

Wallace, Ernest, and E. Adamson Hoebel. *The Comanches: Lords of the South Plains*. Norman: Oklahoma UP, 1952.

Webb, Walter Prescott. *The Great Plains*. Waltham, Massachusetts: Blaisdell, 1959.

Westbrook, Max. "The Authentic Western." *Western American Literature* 13 (1978): 213–25.

OTHER REVIEWS OF CAPPS'S WORKS

The Brothers of Uterica

Best Sellers 27 (1 January 1968): 388.
Booklist 64 (15 December 1967): 490.
Kirkus Review 35 (1 September 1967): 1070.
Library Journal 92 (1 November 1967): 4026.
Publishers Weekly 192 (11 September 67): 66.

The Great Chiefs

American West 13 (May 1976): 55.

The Indians

American West 13 (May 1976): 54.

Sam Chance

Best Sellers 24 (15 March 1965): 478.
Library Journal 90 (15 February 1965): 893.
New York Times Book Review (4 April 1965): 32.
New York Tribune 124 (12 March 1965): 23.
Saturday Review 48 (27 March 1965): 30.

The Trail to Ogallala
Best Sellers 24 (15 May 1964): 71.
Book Week (30 August 1964): 14.
Choice 1 (June 1965): 477.
Library Journal 89 (15 April 1964): 1775.
New York Tribune Book Review (21 June 1964): 33.

The True Memoirs of Charley Blankenship
Best Sellers 32 (1 August 1972): 202.
Booklist 69 (1 September 1972): 31.
Book World 6 (9 July 1972): 6.
Kirkus Review 40 (1 April 1972): 437.
Library Journal 97 (15 September 1972): 270.
Library Journal 97 (15 December 1972): 4058.
Publishers Weekly 201 (10 April 1972): 52.

The Warren Wagontrain Raid
Best Sellers 34 (1 May 1974): 65.
Booklist 70 (1 May 1974): 972.
Kirkus Review 41 (15 December 1973): 1385.
Library Journal 99 (15 February 1974): 481.
New Republic 170 (18 May 1974): 31.
Publishers Weekly 204 (17 December 1973): 37.

The White Man's Road
Best Sellers 29 (15 October 1969): 259.
Booklist 66 (15 January 1970): 598.
Kirkus Review 37 (1 August 1969): 792.
Literary Journal 94 (1 September 1969): 2952.
Publishers Weekly 196 (July 1969): 52.
Publishers Weekly 198 (5 October 1970): 64.

Woman Chief
Booklist 76 (15 October 1979): 330.
Publishers Weekly 216 (16 July 1979): 57.

A Woman of the People
Booklist 62 (1 April 1966): 750.
Books Today 37 (April 1966): 554.
Kirkus Review 34 (1 January 1966): 29.
Library Journal 91 (15 April 1966): 2228.
Publishers Weekly 189 (7 January 1966): 129.
Saturday Review 49 (19 March 1966): 39.

INDEX